92.95 +
rh

PRINCETON SERIES ON THE MIDDLE EAST

Bernard Lewis and Heath W. Lowry, Editors

THE HERITAGE OF CENTRAL ASIA

TO MY GRANDCHILDREN

# The Heritage of Central Asia

## From Antiquity to the Turkish Expansion

RICHARD N. FRYE

Markus Wiener Publishers
Princeton

FOR INFORMATION WRITE TO:
MARKUS WIENER PUBLISHERS
114 JEFFERSON ROAD, PRINCETON, NJ 08540


LIBRARY OF CONGRESS CATALOGING-IN-PUBLICATION DATA


FRYE, RICHARD NELSON, 1920-
THE HERITAGE OF CENTRAL ASIA FROM ANTIQUITY TO THE
TURKISH EXPANSION / RICHARD N. FRYE
(PRINCETON SERIES ON THE MIDDLE EAST)
INCLUDES BIBLIOGRAPHICAL REFERENCES.
ISBN 1-55876-110-1 (HC: ALK. PAPER)  ISBN 1-55876-111-X (PB: ALK. PAPER)
1. ASIA, CENTRAL—HISTORY.
I. TITLE.  II. SERIES
DS329.4.F78    1995
958—DC20    95-45933    CIP


BOOK DESIGN BY CHERYL MIRKIN
EDITED BY SUSAN LORAND


THIS BOOK HAS BEEN COMPOSED IN
NEW CENTURY SCHOOLBOOK BY CMF GRAPHIC DESIGN


MARKUS WIENER PUBLISHERS BOOKS ARE PRINTED
IN THE UNITED STATES OF AMERICA ON ACID-FREE PAPER,
AND MEET THE GUIDELINES FOR PERMANENCE AND DURABILITY
OF THE COMMITTEE ON PRODUCTION GUIDELINES
FOR BOOK LONGEVITY OF THE COUNCIL ON LIBRARY RESOURCES

# Contents

# Introduction

This work was begun in Dushanbe, Tajikistan as an attempt to give an ancient and medieval history of that land. It soon became clear, however, that it was impossible to focus only on the four areas of the country, viz. Khojent in the Ferghana valley, Panjikant in the upper Zarafshan valley, southern Tajikistan and the Pamirs. I then decided that the book should concentrate on the people, the Tajiks, wherever they were found in the past, but that too was inadequate, because of different connotations of the name "Tajik" at the present as well as in history, and in various lands. Finally, it seemed that the proper course was to enlarge the canvas to include all of Central Asia, and to give a history of the various Iranian speaking peoples in the vast area which they formerly occupied before the expansion of the Turkic speakers. Mongolia, the steppes, Tibet and lands south of the Hindukush Mountains, with India, are not included in the present book, and only passing references are made to them as they relate to the oases of Central Asia. In this book, "West" refers to Greece and Rome or Europe, but "west," with lower case letters, is used in relation to Central Asia, and can mean Iran or the Near East.

Before we make any attempt to sketch the history, however, we should clarify whether what we are describing are primarily political or geographical entities, or ethno-linguistic groups. It seems best to concentrate on the last when considering pre-modern history, for the large area, or at least its central part, the land between the present Amu and Syr Darya, underwent many changes in the course of time, and one should try to understand the relations between land and people in the best framework available. The peoples should be recognized by some basic identification, under which different groups—pastoralists or settled, mountaineers or

3

plainsmen, etc.—can be classified. In my opinion the most appropriate criterion for determining the identity of a people is language. But the same people may live in areas separated and scattered from one another, and this was true of the Iranian speaking peoples in the past. In this case, however, one must choose between all of the outlying areas where they once lived, or only that region where they are now predominant.

Obviously much more must be taken into account in explaining the evolution of the peoples whose remnants are the Tajiks in Central Asia, as well as the present-day Iranian speaking inhabitants of the Pamirs. Many times in the past half century I have emphasized that at present the peoples of Central Asia, whether Iranian or Turkic speaking, have one culture, one religion, one set of social values and traditions with only language separating them. Furthermore, I believe that the contemporary culture and customs of the inhabitants of all of Central Asia cannot be ignored in our assessment of the past, for much in culture has been preserved in one or more of those peoples. Many years ago a long since departed friend, H.H. von der Osten, an archaeologist who excavated the Hittite capital of Boghaz Köy, related how at a reception in Ankara he was congratulated by Mustafa Kemal Atatürk on recovering the past of his ancestors. Von der Osten was about to protest, but an unseen kick by the German ambassador restricted his comment to "Yes, your excellency." Afterwards everyone derided the Turkish leader for his remarks. In my opinion, however, Atatürk essentially was correct, for the inhabitants of the present Turkish republic have two areas to claim for their roots: the land of Anatolia and the Altai mountains of Inner Asia, both of which provided much to form the present Turkish people and their culture. Likewise, the people of contemporary Central Asia have roots in the valleys, deserts, and mountains of that area, as well as in the wider Iranian world to the west, and in the steppes of Inner Asia. I suggest that even in this work, concerning the ancient history of Central Asia, one cannot ignore either the massive influences of Islam and the Arabs or the contributions of the Turkic peoples to the present amalgam which is Central Asia. For much that was pre-Islamic has survived among various inhabitants of the vast area, such as new year's practices. Sometimes, however, it is difficult to disentangle the various threads of language, culture, and popular beliefs and to trace their roots, but always the emphasis is on the ancient heritage before the coming of Arabs and Turks. On the other hand, I have extended the scope of this book to include the Arab conquests and their rule in Central Asia to the rise of the last Iranian dynasty of the Samanids and the establishment of Turkish rule in the eleventh century. My reason for this extension is the belief that only with the creation of an eastern Iranian Islamic culture, the literary expression of which was the New Persian language written in the Arabic alphabet, can we say that the new order was firmly established and the past was absorbed into it.

The present Tajik language is a dialect of the tongue of Fars province in the present country of Iran, which provides one example why we must also be concerned with lands to the west of Central Asia in this book. To repeat, Central Asia in this book means the core areas of both sides of the Amu and Syr Darya, as well as briefly the oases of the Taklamakan desert of present Xinjiang, since they were so profoundly influenced by their kinsmen to the west. Much less attention will be paid to the steppes of present Kazakhstan or that part of Xinjiang north of the T'ien Shan range, although both the Ili valley in the east and the Issyk Kul region in the west were important areas linked to the southern regions. South Russia and Inner Asia (Mongolia, Tibet, and areas outside of the oases) will not form part of the present work.

Although anthropologists would flinch at the indiscriminate use of nomads and herdsmen almost as synonyms, what is of concern here is the distinction between steppe and sown, rather than between herdsmen who move only short distances in spring and fall, and at other seasons may live in villages, and nomads who dwell in tents and are characterized by being on the move. The displacement of tribes, or their conquest of settled areas, is naturally important for the historian, so much so that it has often been said that for this

5

vast area history is only made by the movement and actions of nomadic tribes and their impact on settled areas.

Since geography—the mountains, oases, deserts, rivers, and in this region canals—plays such an important role in the lives of people in Central Asia, more attention must be devoted to this aspect of both past and present than in other parts of the world. The present work seeks to help explain the present by surveying the past, with an understanding, however, that a knowledge of the present is also of great importance in reconstructing the past.

Any history, of course, overwhelmingly uses written sources, but the results of archaeology, linguistics, ethnography, and folklore cannot be neglected in studying the past of this part of the world, primarily because the written sources are so few and sparse in their information. Of necessity much will be impressionistic, but hopefully any suggestions offered will be based on as much data as is available, interpreted with a sense of logic, common sense, and probability. Disputed theories will be presented, and not one or the other presented as fact, although I may add an observation that a certain theory currently is accepted by most scholars. For differences in interpreting the past of Central Asia abound, and only the patently absurd contentions will be omitted. For example, J.N. Khlopin's idea that Zoroaster's birthplace and sphere of activity was limited to present day Turkmenistan, where he seeks to identify village place names with the few mentioned in the Avesta, is as unacceptable as Kamal Salibi's attempt to place Israel's ancient homeland in modern Hijaz. Obviously the discovery of new evidence, such as inscriptions or artifacts from excavations, may change opinions presented here, but I hope that this work will be of use to all seeking knowledge about this fascinating part of the world.

This concise and general book is not written from the perspective of any particular part of the area, but seeks to present as much general information as possible about the whole, although obviously some areas are better known than others. Over the past thirty-five years I have travelled to Central Asia seven times, and spent 1990–91 in Dushanbe, Tajikistan, teaching the ancient history of Iran and Central

Asia at the University of Tajikistan. I hope that perspectives based upon actual experience with the people and the land, as well as visiting various archaeological sites, will give a dimension to the work more than that gained from solely reading written material in a library. The meager bibliography in the footnotes is not meant to be more than a very small guide to further reading, for the various encyclopedias of the former Soviet republics of Central Asia contain many entries of use to the researcher, as does the *Encyclopaedia Iranica,* where further bibliographies to special subjects may be found. Many monographs, the *Cambridge History of Iran*, the *Cambridge History of Early Inner Asia,* and the invaluable *Abstracta Iranica* of Paris, provide additional bibliographical information.

Furthermore, constantly growing computer data banks, such as the one on Inner Asia at Indiana University, will give guidance to anyone seeking more references or information about particular subjects. Consequently footnotes will be kept to a minimum, and I shall endeavor to present only general works where further bibliography may be found, or references to disputed theories in secondary sources. Also I will not give references to observations which are generally accepted by scholars. For example, a statement that the end of the Sasanian period of history (if not even earlier) saw an iconoclasm in the religious art of Iran, is self-evident from observation of the few extant objects in any way connected with Zoroastrianism, and needs no footnote of secondary writings which discuss this. On the other hand, from surviving pre-Islamic art in Central Asia we find a different picture, of variegated religious symbolism which requires not only discussion but also reference to the writings of Boris Ilich Marshak or others, not because the point of view is not accepted by scholars, but rather on account of the novelty of the investigations. Likewise, diacritical marks, of concern for the specialist but not for the general reader, will be omitted except in cases where they are pertinent to the argument. In order to make locations on maps easier to identify, I have used Russian instead of local place names, e.g. Dzhambul instead of Jambul and Tiube for Tepe. Modern Chinese designations, like Xinjiang, will use the Pin-yin system; otherwise I have followed the old Wade-Giles Romanization, by which I was taught. Change to another system should not present difficulties. Since no uncertain identifications or etymologies are attempted in this brief book, no ancient or T'ang dynasty pronunciations of Chinese characters in the Karlgren, Pulleyblank, or other systems are presented. For detailed analyses of words and disputed theories, the reader is referred to specialized literature.

Although at present it may not be popular, in my opinion the chronological sequence of history is the best manner for describing the past of Central Asia, a little known part of the world. Upon this framework one can then apply theories of anthropology, sociology and psychology in any attempt to explain the reasons for actions or changes in history.

Obviously for a history of Central Asia, Russian and Chinese writings are of prime importance, since they not only give information about archaeological finds but also new theories based on field experiences. Each is the chief scientific and scholarly language of the respective area of Central Asia. Likewise, now writings in the local languages, especially Uzbek, Turkmen, Tajik and Uighur, need to be consulted, especially for new archaeological finds. Fortunately over a lifetime I have been able to read and converse in some of the languages of the area, which I believe has made my trips more informative and this book possible. I regret the frequent use of the word "probably" or expressions such as "it seems," but in my opinion it is better to present the truth of questionability rather than the conviction of certainty when it is not justified.

This book is not a reference work but rather similar to my *Heritage of Persia,* which was written for students and those interested in that part of the world. But at the same time it is not intended only for English-bound readers who would pursue further readings. It is hardly possible to cover all of the latest writings on any specific subject, and I beg the indulgence of the reader for any lapses or ignorance on my part of new discoveries or new theories. Electronic retrieval for subjects, as well as authors and titles, makes it unnecessary to load this work with footnotes in the Italian manner.

Without access to the state Firdosi library and the Oldenburg, Andreev and Semenov collections of the Academy of Sciences library in Dushanbe, this book could not have been started, although it was finished in Massachusetts. To name all of the friends and colleagues, as well as the authorities of the Academy of Sciences of Tajikistan and the members of the Institute of Archaeology of Uzbekistan, who aided me, would require many pages. The simple list of Chinese, Russian, Uighur, Kazakh, Uzbek, Kirghiz, Tajik, Turkmen, Ossete, Afghan, Wakhi, Shugni, Hunza, Pakistani, Indian, Iranian and Turkish friends and colleagues who have helped me, either with information or on my many trips, would require a volume. My heartfelt thanks go to all.

For errors and oversights I beg the indulgence of the reader, and only hope that future researchers in Central Asia may be aided by my very modest efforts here and build upon them. I wish again to emphasize that this book is a *concise* history and apologize for the omission of many interesting details in the ancient history of Central Asia.

# CHAPTER 1

# Geographic Realities

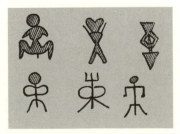

C entral Asia has mountain ranges that rival the Himalayas, and deserts of sand and salt as dry as any on earth, but it also has many fertile valleys and oases.[1] The history of the huge area from Iran in the Near East to the province of Gansu in China—the extended area of topics in this book—is primarily one of oases, large and small. Even valleys like the large Ferghana and Ili valleys can be described as especially large oases, although the boundaries of each are formed by mountains rather than deserts. In such cases, however, a large region may contain what may be called micro-oases, since small stretches of desert or unculti- vated land separate the settled areas. In any case, the impression of living in an oasis is common to all. The expan- sion of arable land was primarily the result of irrigation. Irrigation canals leading from rivers fed by glaciers enabled many people to live and flourish in Central Asia by extending cultivation to the edges of surrounding mountains and deserts.

Although less hospitable for human life than the river valleys of the Nile, Tigris-Euphrates and Indus, since Neolithic times various regions of Central Asia have provided people with conditions favorable for either pastoral or agri- cultural livelihoods. In spite of the fact that the rivers of Central Asia drain into interior lakes and seas, and not into oceans like the Indus and the rivers of China, in the remote past the nature of settlements did not vary markedly between the different river systems in Asia. There is, how- ever, one salient difference between Central Asia and the oth- er regions. Over time drainage of the rivers of Central Asia has created problems, primarily because of intensive agricul- ture and lack of attention to the salinization of overused soil. Today traces of ancient settlements in the Taklamakan

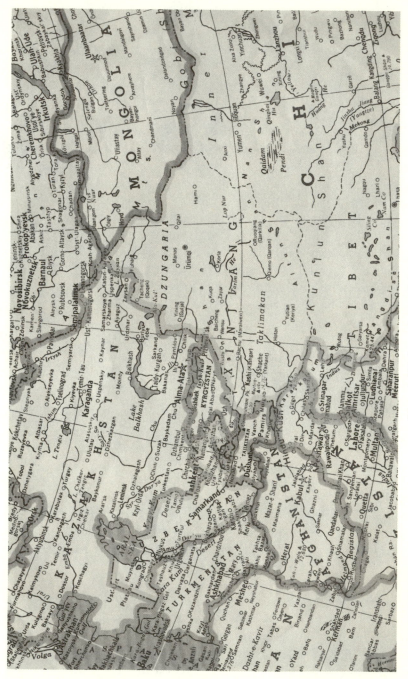

*Map A.* Modern Central Asia

desert of Xinjiang (also termed Eastern Turkestan or Uighuristan), or in areas outside of the oasis of Bukhara, emphasize the delicate ecological balance between rich, cultivated land and the encroachment of the desert, which is a feature of the geography of Central Asia. Water use and distribution from time immemorial have been the principal tasks of government, and also the most important cause of strife, in this part of the world. This applies to herders as well as farmers, for excessive drought can ruin good pasture lands and decimate flocks, forcing migration, sometimes on a large scale. Presumably in prehistoric times scarcity of sustenance was the principal reason for the movement of peoples, rather than attempts to deliberately create hegemony over others for self-aggrandizement. Furthermore, we assume that in prehistoric times populations were small, with enough land and *Lebensraum* to satisfy most of the inhabitants of Central Asia, and with only the spirit of adventure or gain to send individuals or small bands far from their homelands. It is necessary to describe in brief detail just what these homelands actually were and are. I believe it is proper here primarily to use contemporary nomenclature more than ancient or medieval names of rivers or mountains, which I will identify in an appendix.

It is clear that early humans did not have the technical means to utilize water directly from large rivers like the Amu and Syr Darya. Water wheels, canals, and iron tools for creating canals for irrigation came later. Probably this is why settlements along the banks of large rivers are rarely found before the year 1000 B.C.E. Instead, the deltas of rivers, where the spread of water made the task of irrigation easy, seem to have been the areas of first cultivation. Let us turn to the geography of the region to obtain an overview of the various regions in Central Asia.

If we begin with the mountain ranges, the 4,000-meter-high plateau, the Pamirs or "roof of the world," is central to the area. Its offshoots, the massive Himalayas to the east, the principal ranges of the T'ien Shan and Kunlun to the north and northeast, and the Hindukush to the west, with their glaciers and eternally snow covered heights, all determine

15

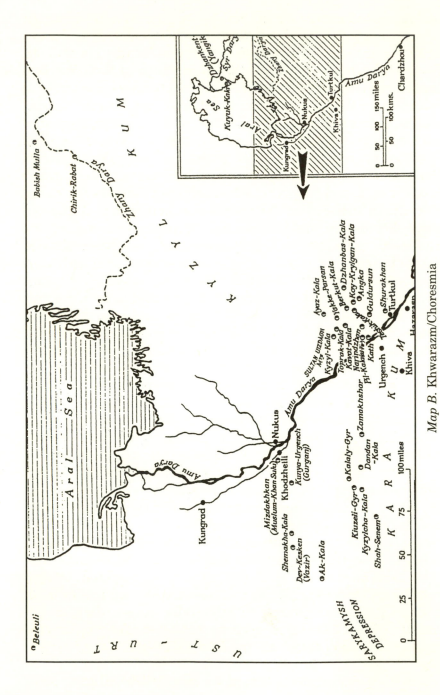

*Map B. Khwarazm/Choresmia*

16

conditions of existence in the valleys and plains through which the life giving rivers flow. Early man inhabited caves near streams and the rivers, and it is hardly possible to determine when and where they first changed from hunters and gatherers to become herdsmen and farmers. Logically it would seem that the most hospitable climate and fertility of soil would attract the first settlers, and, as noted, probably such a region would have been the deltas of rivers, the waters of which were dispersed in the plains on both sides of rivers. Various streams, descending from the Hindukush mountains in the south and from the Hissar range to the north, made Bactria an ideal place for permanent settlement. Although summers are hot and winters cold, it is not as cold there as regions to the north or in the mountains, and the fertility of the soil is proverbial. Probably the upper reaches of the Amu Darya or Panj River, the ancient Oxus, remained the domain of hunters until settlers from the plains moved into the valleys of the upper Surkhan, Kafirnigan, Vakhsh, Kizil and Aksu rivers. Most likely still later, nomads discovered the fine pasturages of the valley of the Surkhab, and of a tributary of the Kafirnigan, under the Hissar-Alai range to the north, with the highest peaks in the former Soviet Union to the south. The narrow and isolated mountain valleys of present eastern Tajikistan, however, probably were places of refuge for people fleeing from the plains for various reasons, rather than choice areas of settlement.

To the north, passing from the Surkhan Darya through the Hissar range to the Kashka Darya, one leaves Bactria for the heart of ancient Sogdiana, while still farther to the north over a low range of hills lies the Zarafshan river valley. In both the Kashka and Zarafshan valleys ancient settlements attest the early settlement of people. Traces of Neanderthal man have been found in the vicinity of the Surkhan Darya, but Stone Age people living in caves are beyond the scope of this book. We are concerned with later times when settlements such as Erkurgan, a large mound partially excavated near present-day Karshi in the Kashka Darya, were flourishing.

Since water is so important for life in Central Asia, obviously the earliest settlements would have been formed on or near rivers where obtaining and utilizing water for agriculture was easiest. Those areas along river banks in foothills of mountains which were inundated with water by early spring floods, or even better the deltas or mouths of rivers which did not reach a sea, would seem to have been the earliest areas for settlement. In fact, archaeologists have found very early settlements in the deltas of the Murghab and Tejen Rivers, and in the Merv oasis where the river dissipates its waters. The same is true of the Kashka Darya and the Zarafshan. In Eastern Turkestan many rivers flow into the Taklamakan desert where their waters too are distributed. The Tarim is the largest river in that area, but traces of ancient settlements have been discovered elsewhere far into the desert, where the waters once reached, but which today are utilized long before they can attain the former cultivated areas. Early shallow canals were succeeded by *karez* or *qanats* (underground channels) and water wheels, but they do not seem to be older than the beginning of the first millennium B.C.E. They were a later development when people saw the need for conserving water lost by evaporation in open canals. As the population increased, people moved from more to less favorable sites in the north, and into more mountainous areas. Thus, settlements in the Ferghana valley, and in present day southern Kirghizia and Kazakhstan, probably were later in history than those to the south in Bactria on both sides of the Amu Darya. Likewise in the north, the Ili valley probably received settlements after they had been established to the south in the Tarim basin. Climate and water supply were essential requirements for settled life in all areas of Central Asia. Everywhere a continental climate of hot summers and cold winters prevailed, with the best areas of settlement near mountain ranges, offering protection from fierce winds from Siberia in the winter and a refuge from heat in the summer.

Central Asia was and is an area of oases, with near or distant mountains and deserts always in view, although some of the oases, such as around the town of Bukhara, are extensive and capable of sustaining many settlements. Many times, however, it is uncertain how much of an oasis was natural and how much was won from the surrounding steppe or desert by human effort. It seems clear that in many oases a constant battle was needed to keep encroaching sand from cutting down the size of the oasis. The long wall called Kanpir Duval or Kampirak around the oasis of Bukhara, and another around Merv, were constructed as much, if not more, to keep out the surrounding desert than to ward off attacks from nomads. Pasture lands, of course, existed in many parts of Central Asia, and herding of animals was always an important part of the landscape.

The steppes of Kazakhstan and the foothills of the Altai, T'ien Shan and other ranges were natural habitats for nomads from early times. How early both herders and settled folk saw the need for trade and interaction between the two is moot, but relations were more often inimical than amiable. Some valleys were well suited for nomads but not for settled people, such as the Alai-Hissar valley in present mountainous east Tajikistan, or the northern foothills of the Kopet Dagh in Turkmenistan. Mountain ranges with high passes could be formidable obstacles for the passage of tribes with flocks, as well as for merchants in caravans, but need or greed could induce both nomads and merchants to brave the perils of mountain and desert, to secure food for herds or riches in trade. Probably the easiest, and possibly earliest, routes from east to west in Central Asia led from Gansu to Dzungaria, north of the T'ien Shan range in northern Xinjiang, through the Ili valley to the west, and then either farther across the steppes to the coasts of the Black Sea, or southward to the Syr and Amu Darya basins. In southern Xinjiang the principal route was from Gansu through Khotan to Kashgar, and over the mountains to the Ferghana valley. Other routes, from Kashgar to the west, such as one over the Pamirs to Wakhan, were much more difficult, and usually followed by merchants only when bandits or political disturbances made the northern routes dangerous. The Wakhan path was taken by Marco Polo at the end of the thirteenth century, but it never was a major route to China. The routes from Central Asia to India too were far from easy, and lack of food and water in desolate and high landscapes, such as

Tibet, Chitral, or the Indus River route via Gilgit and Hunza, would deter most travellers.

Geography, perhaps more than other factors, determined both the cultural and the political map of Central Asia from ancient times. Those areas may be delineated in the following manner:

If we begin with the west and move east and north, ancient Dahistan, or modern Turkmenistan, can be considered not only a geographic but also a cultural unit, primarily joined with areas to the south. Although the Kopet Dagh range to the south separates Dahistan from Khurasan, passage between the two was always easy, and if it were not for the Kara Kum desert to the north, both might be considered part of one larger unity. Nomads from the north, however, frequently entered the land and influenced the settled population to the north of the Kopet Dagh, but much less in the south of the range. To the east of Dahistan there was no geographical obstacle before reaching the Merv oasis, which had contacts in all directions because of its location. Merv was an important center throughout history, and archaeological excavations in the oasis have confirmed both the agricultural and trading wealth of the large region. The mouths or deltas of the Hari (Tejen) and Murghab Rivers probably were the earliest sites of settlement in this part of Central Asia. Irrigation canals were developed here, perhaps earlier than elsewhere in Central Asia, and they contributed to the agricultural richness of the area. Although these oases were well located for trade in all directions, most cultural influences in times past came from the Iranian plateau to the south.

To the east of the Merv oasis is a desert of saksaul brush and sand, extending more than two hundred kilometers to the Amu Darya and cultivation. The desert was by no means impassable, but throughout history it was the frontier between the plateau of Iran and Central Asia, beginning with the oasis of Bukhara. The predominantly desert region of Dahistan was the homeland of the Parthians, whose early center was at Nisa to the west of modern Ashkabad. We must consider, however, whether the great number of archaeological expeditions in this region may have skewed the overall view of the importance of this area as compared with others where less work has been done.

By continuing up the Hari and Murghab Rivers, and farther south through medieval Kohistan to Sistan, including present cities such as Mashhad, Herat, Birjand, and Sabzavar-Shindand to Farah, Neh, and Zabul, we find a cultural unity which may be called the east Iranian corridor, usually in history connected with western Iran across the Dasht-e Lut and Kavir, especially in political control. Underground water canals and windmills to lift water from wells were numerous here, but their antiquity is uncertain. The mouth of the Hilmand River, emptying into the Hamun, a lake or marsh depending on the time of the year, just like Merv to the north, was also an early place of settlement.

The Hindukush mountains of present Afghanistan, the sources of the Hari, Hilmand and Arghandab rivers, probably were settled later than the lowlands since trade, or more importantly refuge from governments or oppression in the lowlands, would be the main factors inducing people to settle in such high valleys as Bamiyan and Ghazni. We may presume that the Kabul-Kohdaman valleys were meeting grounds of Iranians and Indians, with the culture of the latter predominant in early times. The high Hindukush range was such an obstacle to passage that the ancient Iranian name for the mountains was "higher than the eagle," Pairi Uparisaena in the Avesta, and Paropamisus for the Greeks. The mountains north of present Kabul formed the boundary or watershed between streams flowing south to the Indus and north to the Amu Darya. In the mountainous areas of present Afghanistan, the joined Kabul-Kohdaman valleys were the largest and richest in agriculture. Control of this region, many times in the past, provided a base for invasion of the Indian lowlands.

The lands to the north of the Hindukush mountains and south of the Hissar range, crossed by the Amu Darya, comprised ancient Bactria. Its eastern limits were the mountain regions of Badakhshan and the Pamirs, while to the west the Kara Kum desert extended an arm to the southeast between

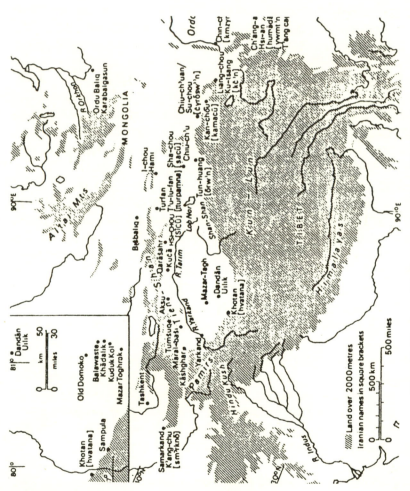

*Map C.* Eastern Turkestan (modern Xinjiang)

Merv and the center of Bactria, the city of Balkh. To the north, valleys of many streams flowing into the Amu Darya provided rich land for settlers. Although one may separate Bactria into a northern and a southern part, separated by the river, culturally speaking the river was not a barrier. The Greeks called Bactria the land of a thousand cities, and the many mounds or *tepes* dotting the valley of the Surkhan Darya and the plain of present northern Afghanistan support the ancient designation.

The easiest route from Bactria to the north, through the low Hissar mountains to the valley of the Kashka Darya, led through the pass called "the Iron Gate" near the settlement of Derbent. The name probably derived from a massive gate installed in the walls by the Kushans to protect the heartland of their empire from the north. The Kashka and the Zarafshan Rivers both rose in the mountains to the east and lost their waters in the earth before reaching the Amu Darya. This was the southern part of the homeland of the Sogdians, whose last linguistic descendants still live in a remote valley in the eastern mountains on the Yaghnob stream in present Tajikistan.

The central heartland of the Sogdians was the valley of the Zarafshan River, with early settlements along the banks of the river and at the delta in the oasis of Bukhara. In historic times the water of the river never reached the Amu Darya but was dissipated in a wide delta. Much of this delta was swamp land, which was excellent for hunting and fishing but required much drainage before agriculture could prosper. The drainage and canalization of the area required much organized labor, which presupposes governmental direction. It seems that this had not happened before the time of Alexander of Macedonia. The city of Marakanda, present Samarkand also called Afrasiyab, was the main city of the Sogdians from earliest times, and it remained the strategic and mercantile capital in later periods because of its location on roads leading in all directions.

Between the ancient city of Samarkand and the Ferghana valley is an arid plain, which narrows to a pass between an extension of the T'ien Shan range to the north and the

Turkestan range to the south. Between the two ranges on the Syr Darya lies the town of Khojent, the doorway to the rich eastern part of the Ferghana valley. To the southwest of Khojent, in the northern foothills of the Turkestan range, is located ancient Ustrushana, which extended over the mountains to the upper reaches of the Zarafshan. The Ferghana valley, protected on the north and south by high mountains, and watered by many streams and a large river, was colonized early by the Sogdians, whose merchants travelled through the valley on their way to China and Mongolia.

Following the Syr Darya towards its mouth in the Aral Sea, we come to the plain of Chach, or modern Tashkent, which also developed in ancient times into an area of settlements. Some of the mountain valleys to the east have extensive pasture lands, which would attract nomads, while to the west is desert. Chach was also settled early by the Sogdians, who brought their customs and language to the area. Finally to the south of the Aral Sea is the land of Khwarazm, or Choresmia, surrounded by deserts, which isolated it from other regions and later made the development of an independent centralized kingdom possible. The question of the course of the Amu Darya has exercised scholars for more than a century, but archaeological surveys indicate that the river also flowed into the Caspian Sea through the Uzboi, or at least only into the Uzboi, as well as to the Aral Sea, in various periods of time. From the 7th century B.C.E. to the 4th C.E., according to archaeologists, no water flowed to the Uzboi but only to the Aral Sea. In the period when presumably the river did flow to the Caspian, objects from the Caucasus area were traded to Khwarazm where they have been found.

The vast lands to the north and northwest of Chach (Tashkent) and Khwarazm were mostly desert, and led to the steppes of Kazakhstan and South Russia. Any tribe coming to the south from the steppes usually would move eastward up the Syr Darya to Chach rather than south to Khwarazm. Farther to the east and northeast of Chach, and north of Issyk Lake, were pasturelands, with few traces of substantial settlements in antiquity. In mountain valleys of the T'ien Shan and in the Ili valley, however, indications of ancient agriculture have been found, although the Ili region is a virtual *terra incognita* for archaeologists. Likewise the southern slopes of the Altai mountains and Dzungaria are little known regions at the present time. Obviously much archaeological work is needed here. Beyond the Altai are Siberia and Mongolia, lands of forests and of steppes, beyond the scope of this book.

Finally, the large Taklamakan desert in the Tarim basin has a series of large oases around both its northern and southern rims. On the northern slopes of the T'ien Shan, near modern Urumqi, was the Uighur capital of Beshbalik, with little evidence of very early settlements, although again archaeology has not had a chance to reveal ancient sites in this region. South of the mountains, however, we find the fertile, low lying oasis of Turfan, the site of many spectacular discoveries of ancient remains in the early part of the twentieth century. Ruins abound, but again much systematic archaeological work needs to be done. The summers are torrid in Turfan, and underground canals exist to keep the water from the mountains in the north from evaporating. To the east is the oasis of Hami or Komul, followed by desert land until the entrance to the Gansu corridor of China is reached near the famous Buddhist cave site of Tun-huang (Ptolemy's Throana). To the west of Turfan was a series of minor oases until one came to the large region of Kucha, which was a great Buddhist center in the past. To the north of Kucha, around the ancient cave site of Kyzyl and modern Bai, were fertile fields, but farther to the west was desert until the Tarim River, where a number of settlements existed near modern Aksu. Farther along the river, settlements existed from early times. Continuing to the west of the river, through desert, one reached the large oasis of Kashgar, which was fed by waters from the Kunlun mountains. Following a road to the south and east of Kashgar one came to the oasis of Yarkand and then the large oasis of Khotan whose outskirts in the desert have yielded many antiquities, since the sand is a good preservative, as in Egypt, both areas lacking in rainfall.

To the east of Khotan many small settlements existed

along the "Silk Route," but the following Lop Nor desert was a formidable obstacle to cross until Tun-huang was reached. To the south and east the large plateau of Tibet lies outside the purview of the present work.

The reason why the oases of modern Xinjiang are considered here is their intimate connection with western Central Asia in culture, ethnicity, religions and languages in antiquity. Kashgar was not far from the Ferghana valley over a low pass, and contacts were easy. From the Tarim basin, the paths over the Himalayas, the Pamirs and the Karakorum range, on the other hand, were formidable, but merchants and Buddhist pilgrims braved great hardships going in both directions, as we know from inscriptions left by them. The vast plains of India, with their spices and other treasures, were a tempting goal for merchants from the north, as were the spices, jade, and other luxuries for traders from the south going north and farther east. One should mention Buddhist missionaries, first from India to Central Asia, and then the reverse, when Buddhists from Central Asia and China made pilgrimages to the land of Buddha's birth. The difficult road up the Indus over high passes to Central Asia was passable only in summer, and only trade in luxury goods with large and well guarded caravans made a voyage profitable.

The oases of Xinjiang, however, were different from those in the west for the land was more arid, and only where streams descended from the mountains could settled life be sustained. Between the oases were tracts of desert, whereas in the west the oases were separated by less formidable ecological barriers, making communication between them easier than in Xinjiang. The oases of Kucha, Aksu, Kashgar, and others were more dependent on their foothill hinterlands for their sustenance, and perhaps more self contained than the oases of western Central Asia. In any case, in the past Bukhara, Samarkand, Chach and Ferghana, for example, were more connected with each other than the oases of the east were to each other. Nonetheless, the culture of both regions was similar and the peoples akin to each other.

This sketchy survey of the geography of Central Asia may give an idea of the terrain and obstacles to commerce, and the movement of peoples between east and west.[2] In spite of physical obstacles, merchants and tribes did move around in, and pass over, the deserts and mountains, either out of fear from brigands or avarice, and the history of this part of the globe may be summed up in two words: trade and water.

## Notes

1. Useful atlases for the countries of Central Asia include the *Atlas Uzbekskoi Sovetskoi Sotsialisticheskoi Respubliki* (Tashkent-Moscow, 1963) and the *Atlas Tadzhik SSR* (Moscow, 1968). Good geography books for each of the former Soviet republics of Central Asia may be found in the series *Sovetskii Soyuz* published by Geografgiz, some of which in abbreviated form have been translated into English. Cf. my book *The History of Ancient Iran* (Munich: Beck Verlag, 1983), 5–6, for references.
2. For further reading on the geography of this vast region see the bibliography in D. Sinor, ed., *The Cambridge History of Early Inner Asia* (Cambridge: Cambridge Univ. Press, 1990), 430.

# CHAPTER 2

# Peoples, Languages, Customs and Beliefs

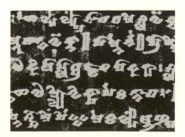

One may determine differences among various prehistoric peoples by their skeletal remains, especially their skulls—whether they were doliocephalic, mesocephalic, brachyocephalic, or the like. By the second millennium B.C.E., however, such distinctions are hardly meaningful, since, for example, in an ancient site like Mohenjo Daro on the lower Indus various skeletal types and skulls have been found.[1] The principal distinction between different groups of people in Central Asia was language, but since we have no language remains, and until the use of writing in, and written records elsewhere about, Central Asia, we must rely on differences in material culture, such as pottery.

It is difficult, however, to connect specific pottery to certain peoples before we have any idea who those people were. Potsherds are the most ubiquitous remains of material culture on any archaeological site, hence they provide the best data for reconstructing prehistory. With all objects of material culture, however, one must ask whether their existence on a certain site implies local manufacture or imports. For, even as today, foreign styles and techniques were copied or modified in various places. Nonetheless, the distribution of sherds on various sites remains a useful rule of thumb manner of distinguishing different cultures if not peoples.

Furthermore, we can use present language distribution in developing surmises about the dwelling places of peoples of several millennia ago. For example, we may assume that the present Dravidian speaking people, of the southern part of the subcontinent of India, extended much farther to the north at the beginning of the second millennium B.C.E. Regardless whether the present-day Dravidian speakers of the Brahui language in Pakistan's Baluchistan province are an ancient relic, or more recent immigrants from the Deccan, aborigines of the Harappan culture probably extended farther to the north than their traces found in the few excavations carried out in Afghanistan would lead us to believe. We do not know whether the Harappans were proto-Dravidians, although it is not unlikely. Did they extend into Central Asia or only establish trading colonies there? If they lived there, did they live side by side with proto-Elamites whose traces have been found as far east as the central deserts of Iran?[2] Or were there other unknown peoples who long since have vanished? We badly need archaeological excavations in the unknown areas, to the north of Sistan up to the present former Turkmenistan border, to even try to answer such questions, but an affirmative answer to both questions is not unlikely.

The aborigines of Central Asia probably were few in number and of unknown identity, although, according to some scholars, possibly related to the present Burushaski speaking people, also called Hunzakuts. But this is mere speculation, since probably some peoples who no longer exist were absorbed by the Iranians leaving no traces. Yet the Burushaski speakers present us with an enigma which needs explanation.

From stories by the Burushaski speaking people of Hunza in northern Pakistan that their ancestors lived in the Yarkand-Khotan regions of Xinjiang, one might suggest that the proto-Burushaskis extended over a much larger territory before the coming of the Indo-European speaking peoples. Burushaski is unrelated to the Tibeto-Burman, Dravidian, Altaic or Indo-European families of languages and, like Basque in the Pyrenees and several tongues of the Caucasus, may be a relic of languages spoken by aborigines in Central Asia before the expansion of the Indo-European speakers. For the latter ranged far, from India and China to the Atlantic Ocean mostly in the second millennium B.C.E.

Thus, before the coming of the Indo-Europeans, we may assume that Central Asia was occupied by a number of peoples, speaking languages which have disappeared, or of which the last traces are Burushaski and Dravidian speakers. Possibly long vanished Elamite, or languages related to Mannean or Urartian, also had representatives in Central

Asia, but the population and settlements of aborigines were probably small and few. It is hardly possible to speak of well-defined towns in Central Asia in the second millennium B.C.E., such as those which existed in the Indus and Tigris-Euphrates valleys. Settlements, of course, did exist, but in Central Asia continuous existing large towns, similar to Mesopotamian or Indus valley cities, are primarily developments of the first part of the first millennium B.C.E.[3] Some archaeologists would dispute this, pointing to large prehistoric mounds in Central Asia, dating before the second millennium. But the existence of towns, rather than several adjoining villages, or a temple complex surrounded by dwellings, presupposes a differentiation of arts and crafts and of professions, which is characteristic of ancient Mesopotamian and Egyptian towns and difficult to find in early Central Asia. Since peoples are primarily distinguished by their languages, let us turn to this realm, and our earliest records are the cuneiform texts of Mesopotamia.

The first written traces of Indo-European speakers in ancient Mesopotamia were those who have been called "proto-Indians" by some scholars, while others, narrowing the identification, suggest they may have been proto-Dardic or Kafir speakers, now restricted to the mountains of northern Pakistan. It is now generally thought that those Indo-Europeans first came through Central Asia on their way to the subcontinent, and also to Mesopotamia, in the first half of the second millennium B.C.E.

The earliest evidence of them is in the cuneiform records telling of the Mitanni people who settled in northern Mesopotamia, whose rulers made treaties with the Hittites in Anatolia.[4] Although the story of the Mitanni is not part of the history of Central Asia, it is disputed whether the Indo-European elements among them, probably mostly the rulers, came into the Near East through Central Asia or possibly over the Caucasus. The consensus is that, even though some of the Indo-European speakers may have moved early from their homeland over the Caucasus Mountains, the main body came through Central Asia at the beginning or in the middle of the second millennium B.C.E. Before the arrival of these people, we may suppose that undivided Indo-Iranians or Aryans came in small bands through Central Asia on the way southward. Both Iranians and Indians called themselves Aryans, and we suppose that they once were an undivided people living together on the steppes of south Russia and Siberia before moving south. This brings us to the vexed question of the homeland of the Indo-Europeans, their probable routes of expansion, and their culture and religion. Since many volumes have been written about these subjects here only the briefest of surveys will be given.[5]

Although the most widely held theory about the homeland of the Indo-Europeans is that it was somewhere in south Russia, in recent years several new theories have been proposed; one supports Anatolia and another has them coming from Gansu province of western China.[6] The Anatolian theory is based purely on linguistics, and is postulated primarily on the basis of the large body of ancient texts in the Hittite language from that land. Although it is impressive linguistically, from the viewpoint of history several questions may be raised. Generally speaking, if the homeland was in Anatolia then we would expect that the first migrations went south to the settled lands of the Fertile Crescent, and we should find ample evidence of their early arrival in Near Eastern sources.[7] Such is not the case, and although stray bands of Indo-European speakers may have ventured into Mesopotamia and even to Egypt, overwhelming evidence points to the arrival of many Indo-European speakers onto the Iranian plateau, rather than into the Near East, only in the first millennium B.C.E. These were the Iranians from the east. No archaeological evidence, such as pottery forms and decorations, supports an Anatolian origin for the Indo-Europeans; indeed it would seem that the Hittites, as the Armenians later, came from the Balkans into Anatolia.

The theory of the homeland of the Indo-Europeans in Gansu province of China is even less plausible, since it is based on two premises. The first is that the Yüeh-chih (possibly pronounced something like *Ruzhi at an early date) of early Chinese sources, who lived in Gansu before migrating to the west, were the earliest Indo-Europeans to be recorded in Chinese sources, and second, that they are to be identified with the speakers of the Tokharian language, a *centum* or western Indo-European tongue, who lived in Kucha and other oases of the northern Tarim basin. Several questionable assumptions underpin this theory, however, the most important of which is the assertion that the Tokharian language is the oldest Indo-European language known, and the Tokharian speakers are to be identified with the Yüeh-chih, even though many centuries separate mention of the Yüeh-chih in Chinese sources and the documents in the Tokharian language from present day Xinjiang. In regard to the Tokharian language, the adjective "oldest" is manifestly wrong since the body of sources in the Hittite and other Indo-European languages is much older than the Tokharian remains. If the word "archaic" is meant instead of oldest, this too can be misleading, since from the viewpoint of grammar (morphology and syntax) modern Arabic is more "archaic" than Hebrew, while German is more "archaic" than its sister language English. Consequently this is an unreliable yardstick for measuring the real age of a language in an historical period. I suggest that until more evidence is forthcoming both the theory of an Anatolian homeland and an origin in Gansu should be regarded with great skepticism, while the south Russian homeland remains more plausible.

It should be remembered that Indo-European is not a synonym for Caucasoid peoples, as contrasted with Mongolian peoples. Peoples with Caucasoid or "European" type physical features probably extended into the western parts of China and Mongolia from very ancient times, but their linguistic affiliations, of course, are unknown.

I should like to propose a simple answer to the "Tokharian" problem of origin. If we assume that the homeland of the Indo-Europeans was in south Russia *and* the steppes of Kazakhstan, and that the *centum* speakers lived to the south of the Indo-Iranian and other *satem* (eastern, Indo-European) speakers, then the *centum* speakers would be the first Indo-Europeans to move farther south. Where would they go? The proto-Hittites would move into Anatolia, either through the Caucasus or over the Balkans. The Tokharians,

*Figure 1.* Saddle cover of a griffon attacking a mountain goat
(first Pazyryk kurgan, 5th cent. B.C.E.?)

as the easternmost group of Indo-Europeans, would move
into the oases of Xinjiang, while others would move towards
the Iranian plateau and India. The *satem* speakers moved
south later, absorbing *centum* speakers on their various ways
of travel. In other words, the *centum* speakers were the first
Indo-Europeans to move to the south and east. Perhaps this
solution is too simple, but it does account for a few of the
enigmas regarding the earliest movement of Indo-Europeans.

If agreement on the homeland is far from unanimous,
most scholars would agree that the combined Indo-European
speakers were acquainted with agriculture, as well as animal
herding, before their separation. This is demonstrated by
some common words in the various Indo-European languages
after the tribes reached their new homelands. The word
"tribe" is used to describe the different groups which migrated to the Atlantic Ocean in the west and to the borders of
China in the east. We suppose that they lived in a tribal soci-

36

ety since this is also the form of organization in later times, among the Germans, Slavs, Iranians and others. In an early tribal society all members had to contribute to the livelihood of the whole tribe, and only the women and older men, who could no longer hunt or fight, would devote themselves to other tasks. Thus the tribe would have two classes, those devoted to warfare and hunting, and those who attended to other, including spiritual, needs of the group. Of course this is a simplistic and even crude picture of tribal society needing much amplification, but the above would apply to those tribes which were primarily nomadic, or at least mostly devoted to herding. Only with the growth of agriculture and a settled society would more differentiation of Indo-European society take place.[8] This brings us to the tripartite division of Indo-European society and religion, of which the late Georges Dumézil was the leading proponent.[9]

Dumézil began with a convincing argument that proto-Indo-European religion recognized three classes, priests, warriors and commoners (farmers and artisans), and this was reflected in the pantheon of gods as found in later Indian, Iranian, Roman, Germanic and other religious beliefs. Others protested that this division was not peculiar to Indo-Europeans, but a natural one for most societies, such as the ancient Near East and elsewhere. Dumézil countered by elaborating his tripartite division, extending each into two sub-classes, represented by different deities with different functions. Thus Varuna/Ahura Mazda/Zeus/Jupiter/Wotan/etc. each found a partner in Indra/Mithra/Apollo/Mars/Thor/etc., the first representing a sacerdotal function and the second a more belligerent function. There were, of course, many ramifications of this simple classification. Attempts by Dumézil and his followers to elevate his theory to a touchstone of explanation for later religious and social developments in the various societies into which the Indo-European peoples were divided, roused considerable skepticism. But at least Dumézil had a model and a theory which his opponents did not have.

On the other hand, all classifications proceed either on a binary or a tripartite division of data, so Dumézil's basic proposals were hardly revolutionary. At present no consensus about his theory is in sight, except the remark above that nomads are generally divided into two classes, but then Dumézil would respond that the ancient undivided Indo-Europeans were not nomads. Even if they migrated, this does not mean that they became nomads to do so. In the third millennium B.C.E. and well into the second, as far as can be determined, migrating tribes seem to have used wagons, pulled by horses or camels, to carry their belongings, and for the most part they walked. If we only had more tangible data about their migrations some questions might be answered.

This is not the place to go into linguistic details, but the theory that the Iranians, or better proto-Iranians, living in the Indo-European homeland, had a rudimentary knowledge of agriculture to which they added much more after they settled on the Iranian plateau, is plausible.[10] In the past many anthropologists considered that everywhere people passed from a hunting and gathering stage to a pastoral one after which they settled down and took up agriculture. This progression is no longer accepted, for tribes may pass from a settled to a pastoral form of life and vice versa. We should remember that hunters and gatherers did not domesticate animals; rather agriculturists first domesticated sheep, goats and cattle, and later probably the horse. Whether it was drought or an increase in wild livestock which initiated pastoralism is uncertain. So the suggestion that some proto-Iranians went from a settled stage in their homeland to a pastoral, and back to an agricultural way of life on the plateau which bears their name, is not at all strange. But to suppose that even this progression describes the history of all Iranian tribes is assuming too much. Rather we should postulate a variety of ways of life with interchanges at different times. Animal husbandry and cultivation of the land coexisted in many areas.

Just as in the recent past when nomads and pastoralists lived around the settled oases, so in the distant past we may assume similar conditions. Also, after the domestication of animals, pastoralists sometimes may have been settled as well as migratory. The absence of food may have caused "settled" pastoralists to go farther onto the steppes and become nomads. True nomads, however, were relatively rare and not in great numbers in antiquity, while before the year 1000 B.C.E. horseback riding, a requisite for true nomadism, was infrequent. We are aware of this from the various finds of horse trappings from ancient sites. Some features, such as the stirrup, are not found until much later. The stirrup, for example, has not been detected before the fifth century of our era.

These general remarks may aid in understanding the early history of the Iranian tribes as they moved southward. Can we be more specific about the movement of the Iranians onto the Iranian plateau, where they found Elamites, or groups related to them in the south and west, Manneans and Urartians in the northwest, and probably Dravidian peoples in the east? These terms, of course, are based on language, the primary marker of ethnic identity, and it is very difficult to attach features of material culture, such as pottery, to any linguistic group of peoples. Nevertheless certain suggestions may be made, impressionistic though they are.

It is now generally assumed that the archaeological culture called Andronovo in present Kazakhstan was that primarily of the early Iranians, although Indo-Iranian (Aryan) tribes before that time may have been associated with the Andronovo culture.[11] The Andronovo people (so named after an archaeological site) practiced burials in graves with timber construction, and they lived in the age of bronze utensils and weapons. From many indications of archaeological sites, one may conclude that the Andronovo culture began in the west and gradually spread to Mongolia, obviously with mixtures in various regions. From ancient burials found in Mongolia, it seems that western Mongolia was occupied by Europoid or Caucasian peoples, while in eastern Mongolia lived Mongolian folk.[12] So Mongolia was the dividing line between the two groups. To the south in Xinjiang, however, Caucasoids extended farther into Gansu province of China. The Caucasians could have been mainly Indo-Iranian speakers, while the successors of the Andronovo people in the succeeding culture, known as Karasuk from a Siberian site, may have been Iranian speakers, since the Indians would have separated and moved south by this time. The Karasuk period spanned the Bronze and Iron ages in the steppes, from the 13th to the 9th centuries B.C.E. Whether the people who lived in the steppes at that time were Scythians/Sakas is uncertain but probable. But based on material remains it is difficult to come to any conclusion, and the record from the Iranian plateau is not helpful in this regard.

In the realm of material culture, however, it is neither possible nor rewarding to discuss the disputes about various forms of black or grey pottery as the mark of Iranians, as opposed to earlier painted pottery of aborigines in Central Asia and on the Iranian plateau. One would expect objects of culture to move from the more developed towns of Mesopotamia to the plateau and into Central Asia, so the diffusion of art objects in bronze as well as clay should not be taken necessarily as the movement of large groups of people. More likely would be merchants or stray visitors who would bring with them prized objects wherever they travelled, which objects were then copied. In other words, invasions should not be the sole answer to the spread of objects, which were sought in trade, and are then found in excavated tombs or settlements in Central Asia and elsewhere. Can later written sources help in reconstructing a history of the Indo-Iranian tribes before and after their separation?

If we interpolate from the hymns of the *Rigveda* and some of the *Yashts* of the Avesta, the picture we gain of the ancient Indo-Iranians is one of rather fierce tribesmen with warriors riding in war chariots and spreading devastation wherever they went, much as later the Vikings. The consensus is that they were not strict nomads but herdsmen who knew something about agriculture. In the oases of southern Central Asia they found large settlements, presumably with elements of culture more developed than their own. One may ask what the invaders brought with them and what did they adapt from the native population? Here comparisons with other Indo-European peoples becomes significant. For example, since we find cremation as a form of disposal of corpses in ancient Greece, Scandinavia, and India, we may conclude that this was an inheritance from undivided Indo-European times. So the later Iranian method of exposure of bodies to vultures and animals may be a practice they adopted from native or aboriginal peoples in Central Asia. This is, of course, speculative, as are many etymologies of words relating to disposal of the dead proposed by linguists. Obviously words were borrowed by different tongues, even between different families of languages, and one would expect very early borrowings between proto-Iranian and proto-Uralic and Altaic languages, as has been demonstrated by several studies.[13] In short, the contacts between proto-Iranians and other peoples of northern Asia indicate that the homeland of the Indo-Iranians, as of the Indo-Europeans earlier, is to be sought in south Russia and Kazakhstan.

It is not possible here to discuss the many finds of objects and buildings, in the multitude of prehistoric archaeological sites in Central Asia, Afghanistan or Iran, for the picture is far from clear about the identity of those who created the objects. Over long periods of time various facets of culture may be distinguished, but the picture we have of that early time is quite uncertain. Hopefully the vast amount of material from excavations will be correlated in the future to give us a better picture of the ancient past.

We should depart from our chronological sequence to examine some general propositions regarding the peoples of Central Asia from early times almost to the present. It is known that in historic times continuous conflicts between nomads and settled folk dominated the scene in Central Asia, and we should examine some of the differences between the two. This is projecting into the distant past some insights gained from much later times, which is always hazardous, but they may be of some relevance. Regular patterns emerged in the relations between the steppe and the sown, and they may be summarized in the following manner: The nomads expanded their power through conquest by confederation, or the joining of a defeated tribe with that of the victor. The Islamic system of *mawali* or clients, at the time of the Arab conquests in the seventh century of our era, might be called an example of confederation. It was unimportant whether this was accomplished by force or persuasion, for the result was the same: allegiance of one clan or tribe to another, usually the result of one leader's capability or charisma. This was true especially in Central Asia, where the cult of the personality of a leader seems to have occupied the dominant position in rule of a "state." Yet in Central Asia the idea of a charismatic clan, destined to rule, developed early, and seems to have been the basis for any claim by a member of the clan to leadership over the entire people. Of course the personal qualities of the leader were most important in securing the allegiance of others. But how did a leader come to power on the steppes, and what were the conditions for his success?

I believe it is significant to distinguish two kinds of tribesmen, at least in their reactions to attempts to create a state or empire. The difference is best seen at the present day in the attitudes of Baluch tribesmen towards their leader or *khan,* as contrasted with the position of Pathan or Afghan tribesmen towards their leaders. In the case of both, however, we find the general premise that leaders usually arise in those clans which have provided leadership in the past, and have a tradition of rule recognized by all tribesmen. In a particular, or recognized as important, Baluch clan or family, an individual has a right to rule by his status in the clan, although by means of his charisma and abilities he has good chances of both securing leadership over others in his own clan, as well as securing the allegiance of others in other clans or tribes to his right to rule them. There was no assembly or election of a chief, as far as can be determined. Everyone expected a member of a certain clan to assert his qualities, and his followers would then obey him implicitly.

On the other hand, among the Pathans an organized or formal council of various tribal chiefs provided the legitimacy of rule, and sometimes the basis for the creation of a state. In the case of the Pathans the institution of a *loya jirga,* or "great assembly" (in Pashtu), parallels the *quriltay* of the Mongols or the *janki* of the Timurids. These councils or assemblies limited the power of a leader, who in one sense was "elected" by the assembly. The term "tanistry" used of old Irish kingship may well fit the process in Central Asia, by which leadership supposedly went to that member of a clan best qualified to lead others in battle and obtain booty from settled states. Tribesmen did not follow their leader unquestioningly, like the Baluch, but were critical of his actions if he failed in their expectations.

In a settled state or empire, however, the most important, or at least obvious, characteristic of rule is and was the bureaucracy, the counterpart to the ongoing or "imperial" clan, when a steppe empire is formed by a tribal leader. What keeps the bureaucracies in existence other than the expected desire of institutions to continue, and usually to expand? In my opinion, more than anything else the sacralization of traditions in a settled state provides the impetus for continuity, not only in the bureaucracy but in other features of rule as well. The end result of the codification of traditions usually is obligatory belief in a state religion. In China this was the alliance between Confucianism and the bureaucracy, while in Sasanian Iran the hierarchy of the Zoroastrian religion became a partner in rule and administration, together with secular officials. On the steppes we rarely, if ever, find at any time a "state religion," rather a choice of beliefs existed. This is usually expressed as the traditional indifference of nomads to the demands of organized religions. In any case, the contrast between the steppe and the sown in this regard is clear.

The settled states, especially China and Iran, on the other hand, accepted rulers with few if any restrictions or sanctions on their authority, since they were viceroys of the gods on earth, descended from the gods, or at least they had godlike qualities. Society remained unchanged for centuries, for stability was paramount in a settled state. If the ruler and his descendants protected the people, and insured justice to all, everything was well. But if the ruler became irresponsible and injustice became rampant, his subjects might revolt, since the mandate of rule had left the ruler. The ruler could be changed, but the system, and especially the bureaucracy, continued as before. The perennial fear of anarchy in a settled state, however, at times led to irresponsibility on the part of the ruler, and consequently the same feeling among his subjects towards the government. On the whole, in settled empires we find a desire for continuity by rulers and ruled, and consequently a lack of change in the structure of both state and society. The charisma of the ruler, however, was a potent factor in obtaining that stability.

We have mentioned several times the charisma of a ruler on the steppes, but this was also important for settled rulers. In ancient Iran, for example, the "divine charisma" of kingship is expressed in various ways, the most popular of which was Avestan *xvarəna,* Sogdian *prn,* and New Persian *farn / farr.* A parallel word in the Turkic languages is *qut,* "glory," which, however, lacks the religious associations of the Iranian words. The concept among the Turks well may have been borrowed from the Sogdians, but the word for the concept was not taken from one language to the other. In Iran we find the *farr* "fortune or glory" of the land and people, and almost a calque of this appears in the Old Turkic inscriptions where we find for instance, *il ötükan quti,* "the fortune of the Otukan country." In both cases the land is involved, but usually it is the ruler who has charisma. In Mongolian the term *su* is used for the charisma of a great khan which is parallel to Turkic *qut.* Although the various terms seem parallel, was the attitude towards the charisma of the ruler the same among the Iranians and Turks and Mongols? Was it the charisma of the king or of kingship? It is my impression that the institution was more important for the Iranians, while the person loomed larger for the Altaic speaking nomads, as it may have been for the Sakas.

To continue on contrasts between nomadic and settled states, it appears that any revolution or change in a settled society meant a conquest or takeover of the administration and bureaucracy. Perhaps there might be some new directions, but essentially conquest simply meant removing the top leaders of the state, whereas, as we have mentioned, among nomads any change in the organization of power or rule meant conquest by confederation, the joining of tribes. For settled states, conquest usually meant expansion of one's own territory, whereas for nomads it meant conquest of settled peoples, or seizing the property of others. When we examine the economic basis of nomadic states it becomes

apparent that throughout history the great complaint of settled folk about nomads has been that the latter exploited the
lands and fruits of others (i.e. the settled peoples), which gave
nomads the reputation of being anti-productive and purely
exploitative. Not that settled people could not plunder or rob
like the nomads, but the goal of the settled folk usually was
to expand and exploit their own land, hence productive in
their own eyes.

The military support for rule on the steppes is also different from that in settled states. On the steppes the army was
composed of the fighting men of the tribe or the people, Old
Persian *kara*, German *Heer*, or Turkic and Mongolian *ordu*,
"the horde." Settled states, however, usually had professional or established armies of various kinds. When the Persians
established their empire under the Achaemenid family, their
*kara* became a *spada* or professional army. In an interesting
combination of the two (ordinary people and professionals),
we find the institution of slave soldiers in pre-Islamic
Sogdiana, which will be discussed later.

Another matter which we only can touch here is the question of nomadic art, for the so-called highly stylized "animal
style" of gold, wooden, leather, bronze and iron objects, found
in the *kurgans* or burial mounds of nomads on the steppes of
Central Asia, has fascinated art historians for many decades.
The origin of this style is debated, whether from Luristan in
the Zagros mountains of Iran, the Caucasus, South Russia or
Mongolia, but the resemblance among objects from all of
these areas is striking. On the steppes of Central Asia, the
earliest objects portray stags or deer, either alone or being
attacked by a lion or wolf, all stylized. It has been suggested
that the deer was a totem animal, and certainly it dominates
our picture of ancient steppe art.

In the Nart epics of the Ossetes the hero Batraz rides on
a deer, perhaps a totem for the ancient Alans, ancestors of the
Ossetes. In Mongolia too, stone stelae carved with the forms
of a deer attest the importance of that animal in the traditions of people living farther to the east. Horses only come
later, probably at the same time as the beginning of nomadic
acceptance of the artistic traditions of settled people (from

*Figure 2.* Plaque of stamped copper (second Pazyryk kurgan)

Greek colonies in south Russia), when steppe art changes. Yet even as late as the fifth century B.C.E. in the burial mounds of Pazyryk in Siberia, a buried horse wears a headdress of a deer with antlers, showing the persistence of earlier traditions.

Horseback riding brought many new objects, such as bits, bridles and horse decorations into the repertoire of plaques, pins and fibulae of the animal style. This is not to say that the art of Luristan bronzes was identical to that of the nomads of Siberia, but rather that a similar culture or spirit can be observed in these arts. Of course much differentiation in the various regions has been shown by art historians. The twisted, stylized foms of animals and monsters, however, show affinities between the bronzes.

Another aspect of the history of Central Asia can be described as a core-periphery relationship, although all of the area has been characterized as a peripheral area itself, in relation to China, Iran and India. In later written sources about Central Asia one has the impression that only cities were important, and elites lived in them with their contacts primarily with elites in other cities, rather than with villagers in their own land. But this is perhaps a universal phenomenon, with the addition that only elites make history, or have histories written about them. Of course one also could argue that the settled-nomadic dichotomy was a core-peripheral relationship, but then we would have to discriminate between villagers, pastoralists and people in a refuge area, the last living away from both of the others. Another category would be colonists, like the Sogdians who settled in Mongolia and China, and their relationship to core and peripheries, or the colonists themselves could be considered as living in a peripheral relationship with the motherland. Obviously these relationships and feelings had importance, and should be considered in any reconstruction of the history of Central Asia, but it is difficult to use them as a model to recover the unwritten past.

Since we have mentioned elites, a final general remark about them may be of interest. Elites were not only the landed aristocracy or the nomadic chiefs, but in the development of civilization in a real sense the activists or true elites were the merchants and craftsmen, a neglected factor in both early nomadic and settled empires. International trade, then as now, was a vital factor in stability on which empires were built, and especially maintained. Local trade in necessities was important, but in the distant past perhaps long distance trade in luxury objects was even more significant for change, and for the diffusion of knowledge. Markets grew as trade routes were extended and protected, and from the earliest times, long before the invention of money, merchants risked their fortunes and their lives in search of profits from luxuries of far off lands.

We have wandered from our narrative, but aspects of these general observations will come up in attempts to understand the later history of Central Asia.

# Notes

1. John Marshall, ed. *Mohenjo-daro and the Indus Civilization* (London, Probsthain, 1931). The only division according to race is based on color—black, white and yellow, or Negroid, Caucasian and Mongolian.

2. The aboriginal population is discussed in several articles in J. Deshayes, ed., *Le plateau iranien et l'Asie centrale des origines à la conquète Islamique,* Actes du Colloque International du CNRS no. 67 (Paris, 1977). Cf. C.C. Lamberg-Karlovsky, "The Proto-Elamites on the Iranian Plateau," *Antiquity* 52 (1978), 114–120; also see J.-F. Jarrige, "Les relations entre l'Asie centrale et meridionale, le Baluchistan et la vallée de l'Indus à la fin du 3$^e$ et au debut du 2$^e$ millenaire," in *L'Archéologie de la Bactriane Ancienne,* Colloque international du CNRS (Paris, 1985), 105–118.

3. Cf. H.-P. Francfort, "The early periods of Shortughai (Harappan) and the western Bactria culture of Dashly," in B. Allchin, ed., *South Asian Archaeology 1984* (Cambridge Univ. Press, 1984), 170–75; also A. Parpola, "The Coming of the Aryans to Iran and India and the cultural and ethnic identity of the Dasas," *Studia Orientale* 64 (1988), 195–299.

4. There are many publications on the earliest Indo-Europeans in the Near East; cf. M. Mayrhofer, *Die Arier im vorderen Orient, ein Mythos?* (Vienna: Österreichische Akademie der Wissenschaften, 1974), V.R. Curtis, *Indo-European Origins* (New York: P. Lang, 1988), and for an anthology of articles see A. Scherer, *Die Urheimat der Indogermanen* (Darmstadt: Wissenschaftliche Buchgesellschaft, 1968).

5. Bibliographies may be found in the *Journal of Indo-European Studies* (from 1973), in *Études indoeuropéennes* (from 1982), and in *Indogermanische Forschungen.*

6. In addition to a series of articles, the main arguments are presented in the work of T.V. Gamkrelidze and V.V. Ivanov, *Indoevropeiskii Yazyk i indoevropeitsi,* 2 vols. (Tbilisi, 1984), 428 & 888 pp. On the Gansu homeland see A.K. Narain, *On the "First" Indo-Europeans,* Papers on Inner Asia 2 (Bloomington: Indiana University, 1987), 28 pp.

7. See, for example, Marija Gimbutas, *Die Ethnogenese der europaischen Indogermanen* (Innsbruck: Univ. of Innsbruck, 1992), 29 pp.

8. Cf. Dumézil's book *Dieux souverains des indoeuropéens* (Paris: Gallimard, 1986), and the appraisal of his writings by G.C. Rivière, *Georges Dumézil à la découverte des Indo Européens* (Paris: Copernic, 1979), 271 pp.

9. For a survey of writings for and against his theories see C. Scott

Littleton, *The New Comparative Mythology, an Anthropological Assessment of the Theories of Georges Dumézil*, 2nd ed. (Berkeley: Univ. of California Press, 1973), and the attack on his theories by J. Brough, "The Tripartite Ideology of the Indo-Europeans: an Experiment in Method," *BSOAS* 22 (London, 1959), 6985. 10. K.F. Smirnov and E.E. Kuzmina, *Proiskhozhdenie Indoirantsev v svete noveishikh arkheologicheskikh otkrytii* (Moscow, 1967).

11. For a survey of archaeological work on the Andronovo culture in a scientific-popular work, see E.E. Kuzmina, *Drevneishie skotovody ot Urala do Tyan'-Shanya* (Frunze, 1986), 132 pp.

12. Cf. E.A. Novgorodova, *Drevnyaya Mongoliya* (Moscow, 1989), esp. 316–21.

13. Cf. E. Korenchy, *Iranische Lehnwörter in den obugrischen Sprachen* (Budapest: Akademiai Kiado, 1972), and A.J. Joki, *Uralier und Indogermanen* (Helsinki, 1973).

# CHAPTER 3

# Before History

Since history, as distinct from archaeology, begins with written records, it would seem that for knowledge about Central Asia we should turn to the Babylonians in the west, or the Chinese in the east, for any information. Unfortunately the world vision of both settled peoples hardly extended to our area in such ancient times. We must then resort to archaeology for a picture of Central Asia, as well as interpolating developments from better known settled regions, such as Mesopotamia and north China, into Central Asia. The result, of course, is rather impressionistic, but in any case it is based upon finds of material culture.

Until the beginning of the third millennium B.C.E., it has been suggested, the main occupation of people everywhere was seeking freedom from want, while freedom from fear dominated the scene from that time until the beginning of our era. A further general remark has it that a matriarchate was the norm everywhere when men hunted and sought food, fighting wild animals. Afterwards, when settlements developed men turned to fighting their own kind and a patriarchate came into being everywhere. Undoubtedly both the spread of irrigation and the use of iron implements were important developments in the history of civilization, especially in Central Asia, and probably both spread from south to north. But what general information can we glean from the results of archaeology? In Mesopotamia, from the evidence of archaeology, one might conclude that there was a general decline in urban settlements over a long period, from the middle of the third millennium B.C.E. until the new Assyrian empire in the 9th century.

In Central Asia, however, the process of integration, followed by fragmentation and back to integration, appears to be different from Mesopotamia. About 1800 B.C.E., or somewhat later, on the other hand, there does seem to be a parallel crisis in Mesopotamia, Central Asia, and the Indus valley. In the first area the decline of Sumerian civilization is matched in the east by the collapse of the Harappan or Indus valley culture. In Central Asia a similar process can be observed in several sites, especially the important one of Namazga in Turkmenistan.[1] In all places were the causes the same—a decline in the water supply and increase in pastoralism as opposed to trade and agriculture—or was the cause invasions? One can only speculate, but the change from urban centers to villages in all three is striking, and perhaps it was the result of migrations.

This brings up an old historiographical question of independent invention, or change, versus diffusion, which is especially troublesome in pre-written history. Several archaeologists have proposed large scale tribal movements as the principal cause of the decline of urbanization.[2] In Mesopotamia, on the other hand, it has been suggested that hyperurbanization led to a collapse of the culture and a movement away from urban centers.[3] A third proposition, that in this early period there was no real contrast between city and village, implies that there was no great change in culture but merely a decline in economic activity.[4] In any case, there is agreement that a change or decline occurred in the three areas mentioned. Most of Central Asia did not have the geographical unity of the Indus and Tigris-Euphrates regions, and until extensive irrigation systems replaced dry farming, which latter was not intensive, hence with lower productivity and a lower population than in the great river valleys, Central Asia remained marginal in development. The date for the beginning of extensive irrigation canals in Central Asia, similar to those in Mesopotamia, is uncertain, but if there was a diffusion of techniques, one would presume Mesopotamia was the giver.

If one may suppose an influence of Mesopotamia on Central Asia, then a glance at developments in the former may elucidate progress in the latter. In Mesopotamia, from cuneiform sources, one may say that the temple in an urban setting was the first institution to exercise both economic and

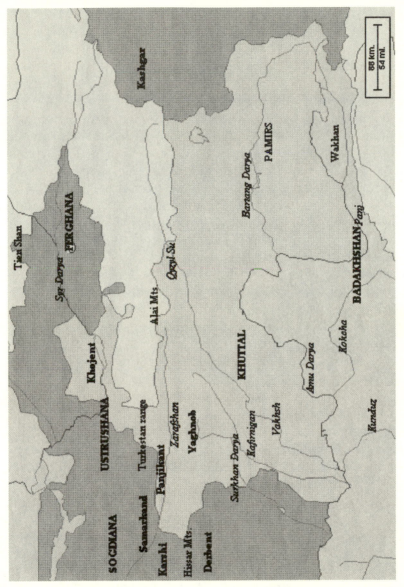

*Map D.* Bactria (modern Tajikistan)

political power. Religious festivals and rites were of great importance in ancient Mesopotamian society, and the temples with priests acquired land, and accumulated surplus capital, which enabled them to sponsor markets and train craftsmen in a community. The religious festivals were also occasions for markets, and temples grew rich in commerce. One should not forget that the temples became custodians of social order and justice, as they also continued to interpret the cosmos for their followers. With the growth of landed estates and wealth, ideas of secular rule or kingship became important, and the ruler came to be considered the protector of the community and dispenser of justice. So the power of the ruler came to eclipse that of the temple with its priests. Whether in all cases the change was from a priest-ruler to a secular king is difficult to determine, but in ancient Mesopotamia church and state became the two bases of influence and power. Was this also true in Central Asia?

It seems that any large building in the Near East or in Central Asia, which cannot be described as a dwelling, is labelled a temple by archaeologists, and any object which cannot be identified is considered a cult object. Furthermore, if an object is not a tool or decoration piece, then the simplest solution is to attach it to some religious purpose. Since many such buildings and objects have been found in excavations, we may suppose that religion was just as important in Central Asia as in Mesopotamia. It follows that the temple with priests should have played a role in Central Asia similar to Mesopotamia. But, whereas in Mesopotamia geography placed few if any obstacles in the creation of a kingdom or even an empire, in Central Asia the mountains and deserts made centralization of power quite difficult. Consequently throughout history, unification of the oases of Central Asia under one rule was usually accomplished by outside powers rather than local cooperation. Temples and priests existed in Central Asia, as in Mesopotamia, but probably by no means as well organized or unified in one system of religion. Of course changes occurred throughout the centuries, but precise dating is difficult. How is one to speak of chronology in the prehistoric periods?

Archaeologists divide the pre-literate past between the Stone Age, the Bronze Age and the Iron Age, and the first is subdivided into the Palaeolithic or Old Stone Age and the Neolithic or New Stone Age, while the Bronze Age is divided into an earlier Copper or Calcolithic (Eneolithic) age and a strictly Bronze Age. This division, of course, is based upon the types and materials of tools found in sites, and the time divisions vary from one part of the globe to another. The greatest change occurred from the food-gathering Old Stone Age to the food-producing New Stone Age, when agriculture and animal husbandry came into use. Absolute dating of the various ages is impossible, but in Central Asia in general the third millennium B.C.E. is the beginning of the use of metals, copper at first, then bronze, while the Iron Age does not begin until the beginning of the first millennium B.C.E.[5] It is not possible to analyze the plethora of sites and their finds, for only general observations can be made, based on the materials excavated, while any conclusions, of necessity, must follow the accepted opinions of the archaeologists who excavated the sites.

We have already mentioned the collapse of the Indus civilization about 1800–1700 B.C.E. together with similar crises in Mesopotamia and Central Asia. It has been claimed that about this time, if not earlier, the very first traces of Indo-European speakers, predecessors of the Indo-Aryans, who presumably came from Central Asia, were found in Mesopotamia. In Babylonian sources they are called Guti, and a few of their words preserved in cuneiform texts have been attached to the Tokharian language from Chinese Turkestan.[6] This is by no means generally accepted, for etymologies of words are notoriously subject to dispute, and since the Tokharians were speakers of a *centum* Indo-European tongue, different from the Indo-Iranians who spoke *satem* Indo-European languages, the Guti then presumably also would have spoken a "western" language. As mentioned above, it follows that the *centum* speakers could have been the first Indo-Europeans to leave their homeland, and the Guti and Tokharians were those who went south, the former to the Near East and the latter to Xinjiang. This is highly speculative, and firm evidence is lacking, but if the Guti did have *centum* Indo-European speakers in their midst, they were few and soon absorbed. We are on more secure ground several centuries later with the Mitanni rulers of northern Mesopotamia.

From the forms of the preserved words or names in several cuneiform documents it seems that the Mitanni, or probably only some of the rulers, were either Aryans (undivided Indians and Iranians), proto-Indians, proto-Dards, or Kafirs, all *satem* speakers. They left few traces, however, since afterwards we hear only of the kingdoms of the Manneans in Azerbaijan, and, to the north of them, ancient Urartu below the Caucasus range, or the Elamites in the south. The simplest explanation of the Mitanni is that their rulers were a small band of *satem* Indo-European speakers who penetrated to Mesopotamia over the Iranian plateau, and for a short time ruled the northern part of the land before they were absorbed ca. 1500 B.C.E. by the native Hurrians (Urartians and Manneans) who inhabited northwestern Iran.

It may be a coincidence that the period of ca. 1700 to 1400 B.C.E. was not only a time of recession or decline in the civilization of Central Asia, but also in the Near East, if not elsewhere in the world. Many scholars would claim that this was indeed part of a worldwide system of cycles beginning with the Bronze Age, if not previously.[7] The next period from ca. 1400 to 1200 B.C.E. was for them one of comparatively flourishing trade and commerce, followed by a cycle of decline from ca. 1200 to 1000 B.C.E. Then an age of recovery and development lasted from ca. 1000 to 800 B.C.E. followed by a decline from ca. 800 to 550 B.C.E., when the cycle changed positively with the establishment of the Achaemenid Empire. The exact dates and the geographic extent of the cycles are disputed, but most scholars concerned with cycle theory in history (or in this time period, *pre*history) generally accept the sequence above. We may ask what this theory does for our interpretation of the past, and what did it mean for the people living then?

Most scholars would agree that the past, as in the present, had times of prosperity and periods of crisis or decline, but the geographic extent of such periodization, and the rhythm or regularity of the cycles of boom and bust, are much disputed, mainly because the data are equivocal.

In Central Asia the testimony of archaeology can be controversial, since correlations between strata in different sites frequently are based only on a few potsherds or other objects of material culture. If a large number of sites are surveyed it may be possible to discern some general trends or threads running through them, such that a pattern of either flourishing or decline can be postulated for the entire region. Obviously a local disaster, such as a flood or an incursion of locusts, could disrupt the picture presented in a general pattern, so one must be cautious in claiming a Central Asian system of cycles, much less a world system. The significance of rapid communication and economic ties of the modern world also may skew our view of ancient times, even though international trade surely played an important role in the economic life of the whole ancient world. On the other hand, areas were isolated from one another and communication was arduous, such that a famine followed by decline in one area might have no effect in another region. Generally speaking, however, a widespread decline from the 17th to the 14th centuries B.C.E. seems attested by the coarse pottery and poor settlements of that period. What can be said generally of the prehistoric period in the history of Central Asia down to the founding of the Achaemenid Empire?

It seems that the geographical extent of agriculture and of urbanism did not vary greatly in Central Asia from the third to the middle of the first millennium B.C.E., except that movements from the foothills of mountains onto the plains increased. The deltas of rivers remained the best sites for the raising of crops, while the expansion of arable land on both sides of rivers was possible almost alone by means of irrigation canals. Channels for water, and ditches leading from them, increased as did the population. By the second millennium B.C.E., in Central Asia most hunters and gatherers of food had become pastoralists with domesticated herds, or settled agriculturists.

Both camels and horses were domesticated and used for pulling carts, while craftsmen working with metal or pottery further developed their techniques and artistic abilities, as may be seen from the pottery made on the potter's wheel. This is not the place to describe the various excavated sites such as Sapalli and Jarkutan in present southern Uzbekistan, Namazga in present Turkmenistan, and many others, since only general trends can be noted here.

The sites in Kazakhstan, such as Syntasha and others farther east in the Minusinsk basin, however, at least should be noted, for it was from this vast area that tribes migrated southward with their warriors on chariots. The Afanasievo culture, followed by the Andronovo and Karasuk mentioned above, points to the spread of objects of material culture from south Russia and tentatively may be linked to the expansion of Indo-European speaking peoples. The Karasuk culture is attested in the Ferghana valley about 1500 B.C.E. and it apparently extended eastward into Xinjiang. Whether a cultural decline of the settled regions of Central Asia, from ca. 1700 to 1400 B.C.E., was primarily the result of the migration of tribes from the north, presumably Indo-Europeans, or more likely a combination of factors, including the salinization and exhaustion of arable land, is difficult to determine. There may have been long periods of drought or other natural calamities which caused a decline. In any case, changes did occur in the centuries of the middle of the second millennium B.C.E. which saw the decline of the Harappan towns of the subcontinent, the Hyksos invasion of Egypt, the decline of the Hittite kingdom in Anatolia, and rule of the Kassites in Mesopotamia. The Kassites may have had Indo-European tribes as their rulers, or simply some tribes incorporated into them. An ingenious interpretation of the ethnic situation in the vast area from the borders of Mesopotamia to present-day Xinjiang has been devised by J. Harmatta on the basis of the etymologies of a few names in cuneiform sources.[8]

In the early second millennium B.C.E. he proposes to find the continuity of three much older cultures extending from the Caspian Sea eastward. The first is the neolithic Jeitun culture (from a site in Turkmenistan), the second is the equally old Kelteminar (in Khwarazm) and the easternmost is the Hissar culture (western Tajikistan). Harmatta contin-

ues that the Jeitun culture was that of the northernmost proto-Dravidians, the Kelteminar that of the Kassites (or
Caspians, *Kasva-, as he calls them), and the Hissar culture
was that of the ancestors of the present Burushaski people.
Although he does not say so, presumably the Caspians were
related to the Hurrians and Urartians. Then, to quote
Harmatta, "The first infiltration of the Proto-Indian tillers
and shepherds into the territory of the Kelteminar culture
might have accelerated the economic and social development
of the western *Kasva- tribes, while their second wave, the
great movement of the proto-Indian war-charioteers, induced
the most developed part of the *Kasva- population to invade
Babylonian Mesopotamia. Finally, the massive migrations of
the proto-Iranian equestrian nomads (Syntasha and
Andronovo cultures), that is, the third wave of the Indo-
Iranians, compelled the less developed *Kasva- tribes to
withdraw either into the hardly accessible mountainous districts or into the northern wooded steppes and the taiga
zone."⁹ His reconstruction is both attractively logical and con-
sistent, although the paucity of facts or evidence makes his
remarks overly bold, and archaeology does not confirm them.
Nonetheless, the movements of the proto-Indians (which
Harmatta designates as the ancestors of the present Dardic
and Nuristani or Kafir speaking peoples of northern
Pakistan) and the dates of these migrations are much disputed, but Harmatta at least provides a framework which
may be revised with new discoveries.

Before we leave the Aryans (or Indo-Iranians) one might
ask what archaeological traits one should seek in order to
identify the path of movement of these people from Central
Asia into India, and onto the Iranian plateau. One feature
associated with the Aryans would be horse sacrifices and
horse burials, or a cult of the horse. Whether this was peculiar to the Aryans, and not to other peoples, is impossible to
determine, but the Aryans certainly were practitioners of
horse sacrifices. Another feature of Aryan ideology was a fire
cult, if not created by them then at least adopted and spread
by the Aryans. Burial customs, another possible index of
identification, are difficult to assess, and they are equivocal.

Probably the Aryans, as other Indo-Europeans, originally practiced cremation, but then burial and especially exposure of corpses are found. As noted, the latter may have been adopted from the aboriginal population of Central Asia, or it might be the result of migration over treeless steppes and deserts to India and Iran. Metallurgy is also an uncertain characteristic of the Aryans, who, some scholars say, brought iron tools and implements into the Near East and India. At least we can say that bronze and then iron implements were actively propagated by the Aryans, especially in their weapons, which have been found in excavations.

Aryans were expert drivers of horse-drawn chariots and wagons and experienced cattle-herders. This is not unexpected, considering the migration of the Aryans over vast distances. The question arises whether the Aryans and later the Iranians either moved to their future homes in a continuous infiltration or in one or more waves. It is impossible to determine this, but it would seem that the process took several centuries and was not one mass migration.

The features mentioned above point to the Andronovo culture of Kazakhstan as that of the Aryans, and later of the Iranians who remained in Central Asia after the Indians moved south. The writings of Elena E. Kuzmina have concentrated on the archaeological remains of the Andronovo people, and she has convincingly traced their movements to the south beginning in the 17th and 16th centuries B.C.E.[10] That they moved on foot, and in wagons or chariots, is indicated by the archaeological remains, as well as by notices in the Vedas about their chariots. In any event they were not horse-riding nomads as in later times.[11]

The process whereby the Iranians spread over Central Asia and the Iranian plateau can be compared with the later expansion of the Turkic peoples, which can be seen in the full light of history. As in the Turkification of Anatolia, the Iranians gave their languages and many practices to the aboriginal population, which in return also gave cultural practices to the Iranians. The resulting amalgam was the picture we see at the beginning of the Achaemenid Empire, but first we should look at Zoroaster and the Avesta.

# Notes

1. On the site of Namazga cf. P.L. Kohl, *Central Asia, Palaeolithic Beginnings to the Iron Age, Editions Recherches sur les Civilisations,* synthèse no. 14 (Paris, 1984), 206 foll. For information about various sites, consult the reference book for excavations in western Central Asia and the Caucasus—G. Koshelenko, ed., *Drevneishie Gosudarstva Kavkaza i Srednei Azii* (Moscow: Nauka, 1985).
2. V. Sarianidi, "Margiana in the Bronze Age," in P.L. Kohl, ed., *The Bronze Age Civilization of Central Asia* (New York: M.E. Sharpe, 1981).
3. R.M. Adams, *Heartland of Cities* (Chicago: Univ. of Chicago Press, 1981), 250.
4. I.M. Diakonoff, "The Structure of Near Eastern Society Before the Middle of the 2nd Millennium B.C.E.," *Oikumene* 3 (1982), 34.
5. The best general book on this pre-literate period is A.H. Dani and V.M. Masson, eds., *History of civilizations of Central Asia* 1 (Paris: UNESCO, 1992), with various chapters on the different ages.
6. W.B. Henning, "The First Indo-Europeans in History," in G.L. Ulmen, ed., *Society and History, Essays in Honor of Karl A. Wittfogel* (The Hague: Mouton, 1978), 215–230.
7. Cf. A.G. Frank, "Bronze Age World System Cycles," *Current Anthropology* 34, no. 4 (1993), 383–429, with remarks by those pro and con, plus a large bibliography.
8. J. Harmatta, "The emergence of the Indo-Iranians: the Indo-Iranian languages," in A.H. Dani and V.M. Masson, *History of civilizations of Central Asia,* op. cit., 357–378.
9. Ibid., 371.
10. Among the many publications of Kuzmina one may refer to "Les steppes d'Asie Central à l'époque du bronze," in *Les dossiers d'archéologie* (Paris, 1993), 185, and her magnum opus, *Otkuda prishli Indoarii?* (Moscow: Russian Academy of Sciences, 1994), with a large bibliography.
11. In other regions such as southern Russia, of course, horse-riding nomads did exist much ealier.

# CHAPTER 4

# Zoroaster's Cult

What do we know about Zoroaster and the beginnings of Zoroastrianism? Basically our sources are the Avesta and later traditions about the prophet. Those latter may be divided into native traditions in Middle Persian (the Pahlavi books), as well as New Persian writings, and foreign accounts, primarily Greek and Syriac. The word "traditions" is appropriate since there is no internal history of the faith but only various stories about Zoroaster.[1] How then do we reconstruct a plausible scenario of the rise of the religion? We learn that Zoroaster was a priest or *zaotar* (Indian *hotar*) of the old Aryan religion, for he is so called in the Avesta. One probably should not speak of a religion as we know it, but in that long ago period a general system of beliefs, rituals and practices would better express the situation in which there were no written texts.

In addition to the Aryan "religion," to use a common term, one may suppose that local cults and beliefs existed, such as divination and the worship of natural forces and objects, for even today, for example, large and ancient trees are revered in various localities in Iran and Central Asia. Just how much these folk beliefs influenced the "higher" religion which we call Zoroastrianism is difficult to determine.

Beliefs are difficult to reconstruct without written "holy" texts, but practices, including rites and rituals, are more observable. Was reverence for fire an integral part of Zoroastrian practices? We may assume this would have been a heritage from Indo-European times, although it should be noted that fire was highly regarded elsewhere in the world. For example, the public hearth fire of ancient Greek city-states was regarded as sacred, and when colonists left for a new settlement they brought fire from the mother city to rekindle in the new settlement of the colonists. The aboriginal population of Central Asia and Iran probably used altars, and fire altars should not be considered the exclusive domain of Zoroastrians, as some archaeologists have proposed.

Since the Iranians migrated to their later homelands, and since Herodotus (I.132) says the Persians did not erect temples or statues to their deities, we may conclude that they originally did not have temples and performed their religious services in the open air. Temples of the aboriginal population existed, however, when the Iranians spread over the land, inasmuch as archaeologists have found remains of temples from the third millennium B.C.E. in Central Asia.

Zoroaster, or Zarathushtra as he is called in the Avesta, initiated some reforms in the religion in which he was a priest. Either he, or a proto-Zoroaster, changed the worship of *daevas* (in the Avesta) into rejection of them as false gods, whereas in India the *devas* were still worshipped. Reverence for cattle, especially the cow, remained in both Iranian and Indian beliefs. Unlike the hymns to the old gods, Zoroaster preached a highly moral faith of espousing the good and shunning evil ways. Such, in brief, is the picture of Zoroaster we gain from the Avesta.[2]

Countless studies have been made of the Avesta and the religion, but the historical circumstances about the rise of the religion are still shrouded in mystery, for we cannot say where and when the prophet lived. It is generally agreed that he lived somewhere in eastern Iran, including present Afghanistan and Uzbekistan-Tajikistan. Theories about his place of origin or of his activities have ranged from Sistan to Choresmia or Balkh. Western Iran, including Azerbaijan which laid a claim as the homeland of the prophet, may be excluded, since the language of the Avesta is East Iranian, and the place names mentioned in the Avesta are all from eastern Iran. No matter where he was born in the east, it would be reasonable to suppose that some, if not much, of his missionary activity was in Bactria, the most prosperous and populous region of the east.

The question of Zoroaster's time has produced even more discussion, which would place him either in prehistoric or Achaemenid times, for the dates have ranged from the fifteenth to the sixth century B.C.E. The consensus is that he lived closer to 1000 B.C.E. than to the rise of the Achaemenid Empire mainly because of the archaic nature of the Avestan language, and the pastoral society in which Zoroaster acted, as inferred from the Avesta. Much energy has been expended trying to prove Zoroaster's dates from millennia speculation, or from a certain number of years before Alexander or the Seleucid era, as found in Middle Persian books. The results are all speculation and none is convincing. Perhaps our greatest problem, in trying to determine facts about the history of the religion, is selecting which later tradition or story has the most verisimilitude. Another question is how rapidly his teachings spread: did they spread slowly like Christianity or rapidly like Islam? It was more likely the former, although it is impossible to determine.

To paraphrase the late W.B. Henning, an old theory is not necessarily wrong because it is old and a new one is not true simply by being new. Consequently, I give here a generally accepted view about the prophet and his message. We should repeat that the concept of an organized religion, with fixed orthodox doctrines and rituals, hardly could have existed in the world in which Zoroaster lived. Rather we should place him in an age of polytheism, where various deities and spirits inhabited lands, towns or certain trees, rivers, rocks or other natural objects. The priests or shamans obviously had no written documents, but relied on memories from their ancestors, and comparisons with colleagues, to maintain any kind of uniformity in what might be called a religion. This religion principally comprised the general practices and beliefs of the Aryan or Indo-Iranian peoples. It had many and varied gods, and wondrous myths with sacrifices which would magically help the worshipper, and of course many folk beliefs were attached. Zoroaster was a priest of this religion, who opposed some of its practices and beliefs, proclaiming instead a moral faith directed to one deity whom he called Ahura Mazda, "wise lord." How can we assume all of this? We must turn to the Avesta, the holy book of the Zoroastrians as we have it today, to seek answers even by interpolation.

The word Avesta probably originally meant "basic (text)"

as distinct from the Zand, "explanation" or "commentary," and this led to the use of the term Zandavesta which really means the basic text, plus the Pahlavi or Middle Persian translation and commentary on the text in the ancient Avestan language. Only fragments of a much larger corpus have survived, principally those which were used in the recitations of rituals. There are large and small fragments preserved in manuscripts, none of which is older than the thirteenth century of our era. These fragments of a much larger original work, according to both language and contents, belong to different times, and naturally the corpus was increased by later additions. The *Denkard,* a Pahlavi book written in the ninth century C.E., tells us that the Avesta was composed of 21 books, only one of which, the *Videvdat* (corrupted to *Vendidad),* has survived in complete form. The rest of the Avesta has only fragments of the old parts, and these were rearranged probably several times in the past. It was recorded in a new alphabet in the fifth or sixth century C.E., which text at that time, we may infer, was the prototype of the remains we have today.

Because of the form of the language, the *Gathas,* seventeen verses presumably of Zoroaster himself, are the oldest part of the Sasanian Avesta. But they are only a small part of the original compositions of the prophet. These verses, plus a few texts which are similar in language, were added to a larger group of texts in a "younger" form of language, which we call the Younger Avesta. In them Zoroaster appears as an historical figure, although he cannot be attached to any event known from elsewhere. The Younger Avesta contains prayers and monotonous invocations of various deities, as well as the *Videvdat,* "the anti-demonic law," which is primarily a collection of purification rules and punishments for breaking such rules. The main parts of the Younger Avesta, however, are the *Yashts,* or tracts dedicated to one or another old Indo-Iranian deity, as well as sections of old stories of mythological heroes, some of which appear later in the New Persian epic of Firdosi.

Just how and when the Younger Avesta was joined to the *Gathas* of Zoroaster is unknown, for the intense tone and philosophical contents of the *Gathas* are very different from the *Yashts*, which are more like the *Rigveda* of India. These hymns and stories of the old gods, against whom presumably Zoroaster railed, were brought into the Zoroastrian religion after the death of the prophet. Changes, of course, occurred in the history of the religion, so that we find a mixture of folk beliefs, more dualistic good and evil speculation, and other features in that religion which finally was codified in the Sasanian period of Iran's history.

The most famous of the deities preserved from ancient times was probably Mithra to whom the tenth *Yasht* is dedicated. He was prominent in the Indian Vedas, and later in Babylonia he was identified with Shamash the sun god, while his importance in the Roman army cult of Mithras is well-known. Much has been written about Mithra, for he was popular not only in Central Asia and Iran, but in Armenia and elsewhere, and we may assume that Mithra could not be excluded from the Zoroastrian religion, but had to be adopted, and even exalted almost as much as Ahura Mazda. Also the cultic drink *haoma,* Indian *soma*, opposed by Zoroaster, found its way into the rites of later Zoroastrianism. All of this is not unexpected, for in every religion older beliefs and practices are frequently accepted, modified, or at least tolerated, and Zoroastrianism was no exception.

In Central Asia, as we may summarize, three general forms of belief and practice existed in the ancient period— first, old indigenous pre-Indo-Iranian practices, then Aryan beliefs and practices, and third, the new faith of Zoroaster— with many variations of all three. An example of the first might be the temples, which archaeologists have excavated in various sites, since, as mentioned, the Indians and Iranians on the move to their later homelands did not have such structures, and we may assign them to the aboriginal population. Homage to fire was a feature of Indo-Iranian beliefs, but not restricted to them, while the *haoma* cult may have been peculiar to the Aryans.

Whether Zoroaster himself introduced or adopted Ahura Mazda as the chief deity of the new faith, and whether he was instrumental in proscribing the worship of *daivas* (Old

Persian form of the name), who then became the equivalent of devils in Zoroastrianism, is unknown, but quite conceivable. Yet some people in Central Asia presumably continued to worship the *daivas*, although evidence for this comes from later times, in the form of personal names and practices opposed to Zoroastrianism, as we know it from Sasanian Iran.[3] In Iran we hear of *devs*, as they were later called, inhabiting the Elburz mountains of Mazandaran, but in Central Asia we have insufficient information to decide whether the religious situation was more like Mazandaran or like Fars, where presumably "orthodox" Zoroastrianism reigned. Of course, as in many parts of the world, popular beliefs in Central Asia included various spirits of water, trees, mountains, deserts, and the like. We have no evidence of any unusual indigenous cults in pre-Achaemenid Central Asia, although it has proven difficult to determine if any existed. Whether the very old reverence for a mother goddess, as surmised by the prehistoric figurines found in Central Asia, as well as elsewhere, continued down to historic times, again is impossible to ascertain. Later Indian and other foreign beliefs and practices, according to paintings and statues found by archaeologists in the region, gave the picture of religion in Central Asia a manifold and syncretic flavor.

The continuous invasion of the area by peoples from the north and east, with shamanistic beliefs and practices, also must have influenced the settled folk, even though details are lacking. One also should not forget cults, with offerings for the ancestors, as among present day Pamiris. Coin hoards found under ancient houses in Afrasiyab and Panjikant, both dating from before the Arab conquest, quite possibly were such offerings.[4] Both, of course, are late evidence, but we may suppose that reverence for ancestors was very old in Central Asia as elsewhere. In the prehistoric period of Central Asia, without written evidence, archaeology cannot provide enough facts necessary to reconstruct the religious situation. Rather than weaving a picture replete with holes it is better to present only surmises as mentioned above. We will return to religion and religious practices later when more evidence is available.

The reader may object to the cursory look given here to religion in pre-Islamic Central Asia since the written material from this part of the world is overwhelmingly religious in content. There are two reasons for this apparent slighting of religion, first, because so much has been written about religion, including much fantasy, that anyone seeking more details may easily find them in various publications. Second, and more pertinent, I believe, is the wrong impression one gains from overemphasis on religion, which is that the people of Central Asia spent most, if not all, of their lifetime in rituals and matters concerning religion. In my opinion this would present a lopsided picture of ancient Central Asia.

There is another aspect of religion, however, which one should mention, for the myths and stories about gods and heroes were important for the inhabitants of ancient Central Asia. We should consider the historical significance of the mythological and epic stories which are found in the Avesta, and in writings such as the book of kings of Firdosi. Were the ancient dynasties, such as the Pishdadian and Kayanian, mentioned in the epic, complete fantasies, or did they preserve traces of reality, even if distorted through transmission throughout the ages? Some of the names surely were real, but again one cannot reconstruct history from such fragments. For example, the name Gotarz in the epic seems to be a name found in Parthian times. The milieu we find in the epic tales fits well the feudal Parthian period, and with the Parthian *gosan*, "minstrels," as the chief propagators of the epic traditions in their time, we may infer many changes and reworking of the tales. Such being the case, fascinating as they are as literature, it is difficult to rely on the epic tales for any reconstruction of the pre-Achaemenid history of Central Asia. It is tempting to try to draw parallels between epic tales and notices in accounts of various rulers in cuneiform sources, but these attempts are mere speculation. It is only with the Achaemenids that we can begin to attempt a history of our area.

# Notes

1. The most complete history of Zoroastrianism is the encyclopedic work by Mary Boyce, *A History of Zoroastrianism,* in the *Handbuch der Orientalistik* series, 3 vols. (Leiden: E.J. Brill, 1975, 1982 and 1991). A fourth volume is soon to appear.
2. The latest translation of the Gathas, presumably the words of Zoroaster, is by H. Humbach, *The Gathas of Zarathushtra,* 2 vols. (Heidelberg: Winter, 1991).
3. Such names as Divdad, "god given" (hardly "demon given"), or Divashtich suggest some form of continued reverence for the *devas* in Central Asia.
4. See Kh.G. Akhunbaev, "Ob odnom sogdiiskom obychae," in *Istoriya Material'noi Kultury Uzbekistana* 23 (Tashkent, 1990), 199–207.

# CHAPTER 5

# Achaemenid Centralization

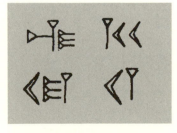

With the establishment of the Achaemenid Empire under Cyrus, who died in Central Asia fighting nomads, a new phase in the history of our area began. Opposition between nomads and settled folk became a pattern for the history of Central Asia, afterwards almost to our own day. For the Sakas or Scythians, as the Greeks and Persians called them, were the first real horse-riding nomads on the steppes mentioned in Greek sources, and they remained the dominant people on the steppes throughout the period of the Achaemenids and of Alexander of Macedonia.

Fortunately two scholars have devoted much of their research to Central Asia under the Achaemenids, Igor Pyankov and Willem Vogelsang, the former concentrating on Classical writings and the latter adding archaeology and Old Persian sources to his domain.[1] As a result the hazy picture of Central Asia in the second half of the first millennium B.C.E. which we have had is now clearer, although it is still bereft of details.

The thesis of the book by Vogelsang is that in the time of the Achaemenid Empire the Sakas dominated the eastern half of the realm.[2] Together with the Medes and Persians the Sakas formed a triumvirate of ruling peoples in the empire, and even supplied the major part of the aristocracy in the east. Admittedly the Sakas were very important, and may have been similar to the Turks in the Islamic period, as Vogelsang suggests, but to conclude that the aristocracy of the Sogdians, Bactrians, Choresmians, and even Medes, as well as perhaps the Achaemenid family, was Saka in origin, is speculative and difficult to prove. What is generally accepted about the history of Central Asia in this period?

To begin with the Medes, the extent of their rule in the east is disputed, and the existence of a large Central Asian

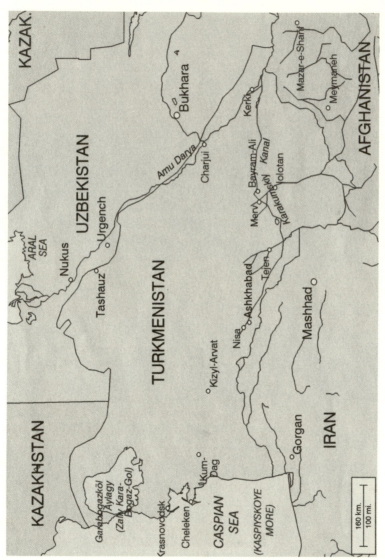

*Map E.* Dahistan (modern Turkmenistan)

state centered in Bactria, which was conquered by the Medes, is also questionable. Reliable evidence, in the form of written records or archaeology, is lacking, so we are reduced to speculation based on the probable nature of political entities in that time and place. Much has been made of a passage in Herodotus (III.117), as well as a fragment (FGrH, I.292), both presumably from Hecataeus, which tells a story that the Khwarazmians once lived around the Akes River, which has been identified as the river of Herat and its continuation the Tejen, and they ruled a large state parallel to, and at the same time as, the Median empire, which was conquered by Cyrus. If the Persians in Fars before the time of Cyrus were still in a tribal society, as we guess from the description of society there by Herodotus, can one expect the eastern Iranians to have been more sophisticated politically, and to have formed a bureaucracy and other paraphernalia of a centralized state? It is of course conceivable, but in my opinion unlikely. By tribal society I do not mean nomadic, but rather both pastoral and settled people, but with tribal allegiances dominating a person's allegiance and identity. Of course, one could expect a certain amount of centralized authority in settled areas, such as Bactria and the oases of the Kashka and Zarafshan rivers, but even similar pottery types in several regions may only attest to the activities of traders in propagating certain styles, rather than the conclusion of one group extending their area of culture by conquest. On the other hand, a similar pottery culture with several other similar objects conceivably could indicate the existence of a large state, in which material culture was uniform throughout its domains.

The main argument for the existence of a centralized state in the east conquered by Cyrus has been the contention that if there had been no large centralized realm, Cyrus could not have established his rule in the east in a short time. This assumes that Cyrus was no Alexander who conquered the eastern part of the Achaemenid Empire in a few years. Yet the fierce opposition in various parts of Central Asia to Alexander indicates that it was not the tightly knit Achaemenid Empire, organized in satrapies, ready to surrender, which enabled Alexander to establish his rule, but rather his military genius and steadfast purpose of conquest over many local centers of power and tribes. I suggest that both in the case of Cyrus and of Alexander local settled peoples submitted to a superior force, in organization or numbers or both, in order to assure their lands stability and protection. Cyrus most likely did not conquer as much, or as rapidly, as Alexander, but he was not devoid of ability to make conquests in Central Asia. Nomads, of course, basically maintained their independence of both the Achaemenids and Alexander.

The story by Ctesias, as reported in Diodorus (II.26), that the Assyrian king Ninus, and then queen Semiramis, fought against the Bactrians and made conquests in the east, is supported by no cuneiform evidence, and may reflect only the legendary (or epic) traditions of the Iranians in relating stories about pre-Achaemenid events in the east. It is impossible to recover history from such accounts, and I would maintain that various reconstructions of the past of Central Asia are indeed possible, but none is even compellingly probable. This does not mean, however, that we can rely on nothing in the written sources to reconstruct the past.

Whatever the nature of Median rule, there is no doubt that they had an army which, together with the Babylonians, conquered Nineveh and brought an end to Assyrian power. The Persians in Fars were under Median rule, and probably other areas in the east recognized the hegemony of the Medes. Vogelsang's suggestion that the word hegemony best describes the nature of Achaemenid rule in Central Asia is attractive, and this could also apply to Median "rule" in the east. Achaemenid control, especially after the reign of Darius, of course, was better organized and more centralized than previously, but the pattern fits both times. Hegemony implies recognition by local rulers of the overlordship of the Median and then Achaemenid sovereign, with personal ties established by marriage or other connections, cemented by gifts. Thus the Median ruler, and Cyrus and his successors, could truthfully call themselves "king of kings," since local "kings" recognized their supremacy, and, of course, they had conquered other regions as well. What of the Sakas, who caused problems both for Cyrus and Alexander, not to mention Darius and probably other Achaemenid rulers?

To apply some generalities to the picture of the Sakas in Central Asia at this time, we may ask some questions. Until recent times it seems that the history of Central Asia was determined by nomads. Both on the steppes and in the oases, the leaders of nomadic confederations provided protection to the settled folk, who paid tribute to their more mobile and warlike neighbors from the steppes. The settled people usually called all of the nomads in a confederation after the leading tribe or clan.[3] Later in the history of Central Asia, all nomads were called Huns by settled folk, although obviously many peoples other than nomads were placed under that designation. (Even the Ottoman Turks who took Constantinople under Mehmet in 1453 were called Huns by several Greek chroniclers.) The Persians had several designations for various groups of Sakas, as seen in the Old Persian inscriptions, while the Greeks give us a number of tribal names of the Scythians, few of which unfortunately can be identified with the Persian names. I must confess to an inability to use the notices in the Avesta (especially Yasht XIII.143) about peoples called Tura, Sairima, Saini and Danha, since even guesses about their identity do not help us in reconstructing history. One may suggest that they were Saka tribes, but even that is subject to dispute. Since the Persians were better acquainted with the nomads of Central Asia than were the Greeks, we should look first to the Persian names of the Central Asian nomads.[4]

The names of the Sakas in Old Persian inscriptions are the following: *Saka Haumavarga, Saka Paradraya* (beyond the sea or river), *Saka Tigrakhauda* (pointed hats), *Saka para Sugdam* (Sakas beyond Sogdiana), while an Egyptian inscription speaks of Sakas of the marshes (or more likely meaning "distant"), and Sakas of the plains. The locales of none of them can be identified, and only guesses can be made, for the Sakas extended from the Danube River to Mongolia and south to the Iranian plateau. The Saka Haumavarga have been identified with the Amyrgioi Scythians of Greek sources, with no indication of exactly where they were located. The Massagetai of Greek sources, placed by them in Dahistan, to the east of the Caspian, are called a group of Scythians by Arrian (IV.16.4), and we find other, presumably tribal, names such as Derbikes, but again locations elude us. Where would one expect nomads to live in southern Central Asia, for clearly they also roamed over the steppes of south Russia and Kazakhstan?

Since nomads depend on trade and on a close relationship with settled folk, we should expect those areas where later nomads are found to exist, to be the same locations where they flourished in antiquity, namely rich pasture lands for flocks. The oasis of Bukhara, for example, might have been the region where some Sakas lived. The foothills of the Kopet Dagh, ancient Dahistan, would be another area for nomadic life. Likewise the foothills of the mountains surrounding the Ferghana valley were ever rich pasture lands, as was the narrow Alai valley in eastern contemporary Tajikistan. On the whole, the flat land of Bactria proper did not provide the best pastures for the flocks of nomads; furthermore the area was full of irrigation ditches and cultivated land. Also, one must remember that nomads did not flourish in deserts, although they could survive in, and pass through, them. Since anthropologists tell us that a symbiosis between settled folk and nomads was essential for the life of the latter, one would expect the nomads to have close contacts with the settled people of the oases of Central Asia. But to return to identifications, it would not be amiss to assign the Haumavarga (*haoma*-using?) Sakas to the Ferghana valley and adjacent valleys, including the Alai and Pamirs, while the Tigrakhauda Sakas roamed in a more western and northern region, possibly near Choresmia (Khwarazm) and extending beyond the Syr Darya into modern Kirghizia and Kazakhstan. Whether these Sakas are the same as those beyond Sogdiana (in an inscription from Persepolis, DPh), is probable, but obviously some tribes of nomads did not remain in one area, but wandered at times far from their homelands in search of better pasturelands, or they were rewarded with new lands for services rendered to a ruler. Graves of nomad princes who wore pointed hats have been found in

Kazakhstan and Afghanistan, and these finds reinforce the suggestion that the pointed-hat Sakas lived in Central Asia, particularly to the north of the Syr Darya.[5] The Sakas or Scythians of South Russia were a third group which will not concern us here. Let us return to the Medes and Achaemenids.[6]

Even though it may be true that some Saka chiefs and their associates became devoted partners of the Medes, and then the Persians, as Vogelsang suggests, certainly Cyrus and also Darius had to fight the Sakas in their homelands. Cyrus lost his life fighting them in the summer of 530 (or 529) B.C.E. according to Herodotus (I.205–14), Ctesias and others. The tribal names vary in the sources, and the exact circumstances of his death are also varied, but his death in fighting nomads in the northeastern part of his domains is supported by all sources. About a decade later Darius says in his Behistun inscription (column 5 with lacunae reconstructed here): "Afterwards I went to Saka land with an army against the Sakas who wear a pointed hat. When I arrived at the sea (or river) I went beyond it with all my army. Afterwards I severely defeated the Sakas. One (chief?) I took captive, who was led bound to me and I slew him. Then I made another one chief, as was my wish. They seized their chief Skunkha and led him to me. Afterwards that land became mine. Those Sakas were faithless and Ahura Mazda was not worshipped by them. I worshipped Ahura Mazda. By the will of Ahura Mazda, as was my desire, thus I did to them."

So under Cyrus and Darius the Sakas were hardly partners of the Persians and Medes in rule of the empire. Also the information that the Sakas did not worship Ahura Mazda, as Darius did, implies a certain hostility based on religion. On the other hand, since the nomads were formidable fighters, we may assume that after submission, many did join the ranks of the Achaemenid army, as we learn from mention of them serving in later expeditions of the Achaemenids. Other than the army, however, it is unlikely that Sakas attained high offices in the bureaucracy and rule of the empire. Although we learn of many revolts in the western part of the empire from Greek sources, there is no information about

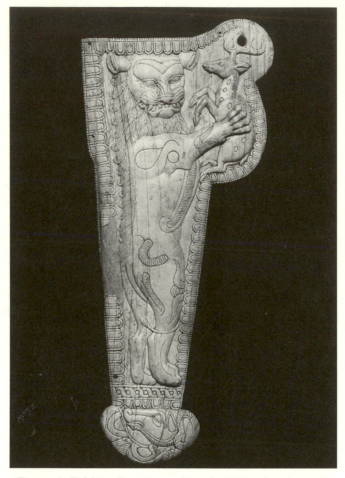

*Figure 3.* Takht-e Sangin, scabbard of Akinakes (sword) with lion and antelope, Achaemenid period

revolts in eastern Iran or Central Asia. This does not mean that there were none, but only one notice exists in unreliable Ctesias (fragment 31) that a certain Artabanus in Bactria (presumably the satrap) revolted against Artaxerxes I, but his uprising was suppressed. In any case, revolts in the east on the whole, it seems, were by pretenders to the throne rather than local uprisings, and surely not by the common folk.

The period of Achaemenid rule in the east is in fact a blank page, and we are forced to interpolate from the historians of Alexander's conquests to obtain an impression of the situation in the east just before the fall of the empire. But before turning to the Achaemenids what did we conclude about the Medes and the conquests of Cyrus in the east?

It is now generally accepted that the Medes probably exercised some hegemony in the east, mainly because Parthia and Hyrcania (Gurgan) later supported Fravartish, the Median pretender to the throne in his opposition to Darius. On the other hand, according to the Behistun inscription, Bactria and Arachosia supported Darius, which implies that they already had been conquered by Cyrus, and had no links to a previous Median control, which is only a guess. Although the dates of Cyrus's campaigns in Central Asia have been disputed, it is possible that they took place both before and after his conquest of Babylon in 539 B.C.E. It is further suggested that Bactria, as the leading land of the east in population and wealth, had exercised either political control, or at least strong cultural influence, over neighboring lands before conquest by Cyrus. Whether there had been a Bactrian empire, or more likely a confederation under Bactrian leadership, before the time of Cyrus, is uncertain.[7] Likewise, the original geographical position of the Choresmians has been assigned to the mountainous area between present Herat and Balkh, with a migration of this people to the north, along the Oxus River to the flat land south of the Aral Sea, at sometime during the Achaemenid empire. This may have happened, but to speculate further on historical causes for such a migration is fruitless.[8] In my opinion, speculation about revolts and reconquests of various Saka tribes, and other peoples of the east, by the Achaemenids, based on the inclusion or exclusion of names from the Old Persian inscriptions, while interesting, in no way should be considered historically proven.

It is frustrating to have so little information about Central Asia under the Achaemenids, and the temptation to spin a narrative from a word in the cuneiform inscriptions, or from an etymology of a word, is attractive but could be misleading. In any case, we can say that inclusion in the huge empire of the Achaemenids brought Central Asia into closer contact with western Iran and the entire Near East, which brought changes to their way of life, as mentioned below. Before we turn to that, however, let us further examine what the Behistun inscription of Darius says about Central Asia.

Two lands in Central Asia did not accept Darius as ruler of the empire: Parthia and Hyrcania (or Margiana as the Babylonian text of the inscription says). The rebels instead supported Fravartish, who called himself king in Media, a descendant of Cyaxares, the former ruler of Media before the Achaemenids. Vishtaspa, the father of Darius, who was satrap of Parthia, defeated the rebels, but the people of Margiana or Merv refused to accept Darius, and their leader, Frada, proclaimed himself king of Margiana. Frada was defeated by the satrap of Bactria called Dadarshi, who was on the side of Darius. Many prisoners were taken, and Frada and his principal followers were executed. From this terse account we may infer that Merv probably had been part of the Median empire, and had not accepted Achaemenid rule with enthusiasm, so that when revolts occurred, they joined the rebels against the Achaemenids. Bactria, and presumably Sogdiana, supported Darius, possibly because they had no previous allegiance to any ruler of the Medes and did not want to disturb the advantages in trade they enjoyed under an empire the size of the Achaemenid one. There may have been other reasons, such as more Persian troops and central control in Bactria than elsewhere. Afterwards, Central Asia seems to have remained faithful to the Achaemenids. The oasis of Merv, we may suppose, either remained part of the satrapy of Bactria or was put under that satrapy after the revolt was suppressed. Did the Persians dominate the administration of Central Asia afterwards?

It is difficult to determine whether Persians filled the posts of satraps in the Central Asian portions of the empire, or whether local Iranian lords accepted the position of satrap, from the Achaemenid king, over their own domains. When Classical sources mention an Achaemenid prince as satrap in Central Asia, however, we do have evidence of Persian rule

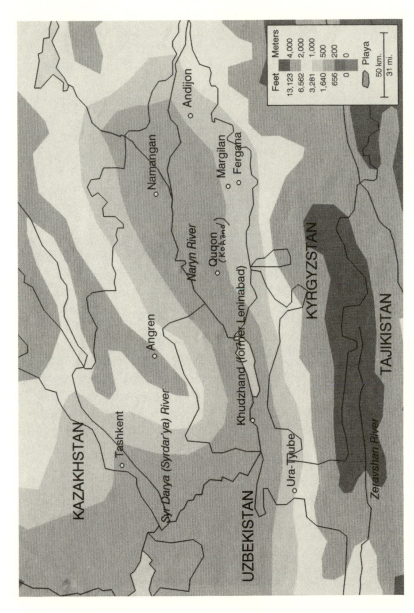

*Map F.* Ferghana valley and southern steppes (modern Kirgizia and Kazakhstan)

over a specific satrapy, as Hystaspes (Vishtaspa) son of Darius I, over Bactria (Herodotus VII.64). We must assume that he, as the leader of the Bactrian and Saka contingent in the invasion of Greece under Xerxes, was the satrap, and not a military commander. The combination of military and administrative functions in the person of the satrap, which earlier in the empire seem to have been separate, is impossible to date. But were Central Asians employed in high positions elsewhere in the empire?

It is difficult to conclude that a certain person was a Bactrian or Sogdian solely on the basis of his name, for parents in the east at times surely gave Achaemenid names to their children, while dialect division in names is uncertain. Central Asians did serve in minor positions elsewhere, however, for we hear of a Choresmian in an Achaemenid garrison at Elephantine in Upper Egypt.[9] Also Central Asians served in the Achaemenid armies that invaded Greece under both Darius and Xerxes, and we may suppose some of them remained in the west in garrisons. On analogy with later times, one can imagine that the upper classes in the Iranian speaking world, as well as officials, could speak Persian as well as their own tongue. By Persian I do not mean the archaizing language of the Old Persian inscriptions, but rather a *koine* which was closer to the Middle Persian stage of the language than to that of the cuneiform inscriptions. Persian customs and styles also probably influenced local peoples, even though the more practical riding costumes and armament, especially bow, arrows and short sword of the Sakas, spread among other Iranian peoples, as Vogelsang has shown.[10] On the other hand, changes probably were limited to the upper classes, since material remains of the population found by archaeologists show continuity from previous cultures, rather than any innovations presumably wrought by inclusion within the Achaemenid Empire. But one should not say there was no influence on the life of the ordinary people, for inclusion within the empire brought stability and far flung trade contacts if nothing else. For example, soldiers of various origins, settled in garrisons in various parts of the empire, encouraged a mixture of information and culture, and Central Asia cannot have been an exception. Let us consider the town of Cyreschata or Cyropolis presumably founded by Cyrus at the extreme east of the empire.[11]

If Ptolemy (VI.12.5) is correct, the town of Cyreschata was located on the Jaxartes or Syr Darya, which makes an identification with a site near the present city of Khojent probable. Other archaeological sites in the vicinity have been proposed for the identification of Cyreschata, but Khojent is situated where the river comes between two mountain ranges and its strategic importance is clear, although possibly only Alexander realized this in founding one of his cities here. Presumably the town, wherever it was located, would have been a garrison place, and as such walls would have surrounded it. Whether a walled town implies an import from the west, as has been suggested by some scholars, is dubious, but presumably soldiers made up a large part of the population of the town. Probably the garrisons were separate from the towns, located in citadels or fortresses comparable to those of the British in India, but unlike the Arabs who settled among the townfolk in Central Asia to propagate their Islamic religion among them. Cyreschata then could be described as an Achaemenid garrison town on the frontier of the empire, and there probably were others elsewhere.

The most important city for the entire area north of the Oxus was Samarkand, where presumably the administrative government, such as it was, would have been located. The largest city and capital for all of the east, however, seems to have been Bactra. Although there is as yet no archaeological or written evidence for the existence of a road and postal system in Central Asia similar to the "Royal Road" from Susa to Sardis (see Herodotus V.52, and traces of the road near Pasargadae and Persepolis), we may suppose that transportation and communications to the east were not neglected by the Achaemenids. Because of the very existence of the empire for two centuries, we may assume many bureaucratic as well as cultural influences from the center on the various parts of the empire, including Central Asia.

This can best be seen in the use of Aramaic as the bureaucratic language of the empire, for the languages of Central

Asia which were later written—Bactrian, Sogdian and Khwarazmian—all of their alphabets were derived from the Aramaic of the Achaemenid chancellery. That is a later story, however, since technical or bureaucratic words, presumably derived from Achaemenid usage, do not appear in texts until much later times. There is no evidence for any system of writing current in Central Asia in Achaemenid times other than Aramaic. At this time the Chinese language in the pre-Han era was still too far away to have been used in eastern Turkestan, although a few enterprising merchants from China conceivably could have ventured to the far west, bringing at least information about their own system of writing to the peoples of Xinjiang.

One policy of the Achaemenid government had a direct influence on the peoples of Central Asia, and that was the practice of exiling whole villages or towns to the east after rebellions against royal authority. Ionian Greeks were sent to various places in the east after their failed revolt, and an Egyptian village was reconstructed in Bactria by exiles according to Herodotus (IV.204). One wonders how the exiles were sent, presumably on foot, with soldiers guarding any attempts at escape. Many must have lost their lives on such a trip over vast distances, and what was the relation of the exiles to their neighbors? Not only were exiles from the west settled in Central Asia, but presumably also Ionian Greeks from Anatolia, and others, were sent there as officers of the great king in various capacities. Some may have remained, but their numbers were small, otherwise there would have been notices about them in the works of the historians of Alexander. It is difficult to say whether the mention of a priestly group called Branchidae, who were sent from Milet in Anatolia to Bactria by Xerxes, was unique, or simply reported as an example of others (Strabo XI.2.4, XIV.1.5 and Curtius VII.5.28).

Finds of Greek coins dating before the time of Alexander could be attributed to Greeks in Achaemenid employ or to merchants from the west.[12] There is no evidence, however, that in the eastern part of the empire any coins were current, as in Anatolia and on the Mediterranean coast. Rather, on the whole in Central Asia, coins probably were collected mainly for artistic or souvenir motives, as well as for their metal content. One has the impression that the eastern part of the empire was not as well organized as the west, nor was central control as efficacious. Likewise, if the great king was able to enforce adherence to his worship of Ahura Mazda among his Persian subjects, surely he was less successful in this regard in the east, to judge by a projection into Achaemenid times of later local religions in the region. Perhaps the saying that prophets are never revered in their homelands would apply to Central Asia. Are we then to assume that Achaemenid rule had less effect on Central Asia than suggested above?

The discovery of a carpet with Achaemenid motifs from Persepolis on it in far away Pazyryk, Siberia, dating from the late Achaemenid or early Seleucid era, is evidence of the far-flung cultural influence of Achaemenid Iran.[13] Undoubtedly in the oases of southern Central Asia, nominally under Achaemenid rule, such influence was stronger than farther north, but archaeologists have not uncovered in Central Asia a miniature Persepolis, modelled after the royal residence in Persis. While a satrap in the east might have tried to copy his sovereign, he had neither the wealth nor the manpower to do so, but the spades of the archaeologist may yet find a large Achaemenid palace complex in the eastern part of the empire. We must turn to the Near East for information about Achaemenid rule and consider possible parallels in the east.

We know that military leaders in Babylonia were given grants of land, called *qashtu* in Akkadian, in recompense for service to the state. Did this system exist in Central Asia? We may conjecture that a similar process did obtain in the east where, however, local lords who served the Achaemenids by bringing their own forces to augment the Achaemenid army at the request of the great king, were principally the recipients of such largesse. The phenomenon of Arsames, an Achaemenid prince who owned land in Babylonia, Egypt and elsewhere, probably was rarely found, if at all, in the east. The local aristocracy in Central Asia comprised the landlords who oversaw the regulation and distribution of water for agriculture, much as in pre-Achaemenid times. As always, water was the life blood, and necessity for prosperity, of eastern Iran and Central Asia, and the region could not compete with Babylonia and Egypt in agricultural richness.

Since there was no currency in use in the east (gold *darics* and Greek coins were current only in the west), the yearly gifts (euphemism for taxes) obviously were in kind, as we see on the reliefs at Persepolis. To bring sheep or grain to Persepolis from Central Asia was hardly practical, so gold and semi-precious stones, such as lapis lazuli, carnelian and turquoise, were preferable. Lapis was mined in Badakhshan from very old times until today, and turquoise at present comes from the mountain range north of Nishapur, but possibly in ancient times other sources existed which no longer can be found.[14] Mining was an important industry in the mountains of Central Asia, and products of the metals and stones, such as cups and bracelets as depicted at Persepolis, were sought by the Achaemenid king and his courtiers. Silver vessels of various design were later one of the main products of trade from Central Asia to the west up the Volga River and to China in the east.

Although the yearly "taxes" were at first only in kind, by the time of Darius I, after his reorganization of the empire into satrapies, their value was reckoned in silver talents, a unit of weight of about 30 kg. In Herodotus (III.89) the geographical units which were taxed together do not correspond to the satrapies. For example, the Bactrians and their neighbors paid 360 talents, while the Parthians, Choresmians, Sogdians and Areians (Herat area) together paid 390 talents every year. The peoples of Asia Minor, Babylonia and Egypt paid much more, but Bactria was the richest of the eastern lands, except for the Indians who also paid 360 talents in gold dust. Herodotus also tells us that the ratio of gold to silver was thirteen to one, a relationship which existed throughout history.

One should not believe all that Herodotus reports, but his account of the taxation shows the financial sophistication of the Achaemenid Empire. Revenues also came to the central government, or court, by road tolls and excise taxes, as well as exceptional levies, especially for the army on its campaigns. How much of the structure and institutions current in the western part of the empire were also found in Central Asia is difficult to determine, but one may assume that most were.

In Babylonia there were numerous slaves of different standing, including some who owned other slaves. At Persepolis, and presumably elsewhere in Iran, domestic slaves were found, but large groups of paid manual laborers seem to have taken the place of slave labor, as we learn from Elamite tablets from Persepolis. There was corvée labor (obligatory service) everywhere, and in Central Asia this was necessary for the maintenance of irrigation canals as well as underground channels. Slave labor was unprofitable compared with hired help, which latter seems to have been dominant in Central Asia. The system of clientship, as we know later among Arab tribes, had several forms, and the nomads of Central Asia practiced it, as well as the sale of children to local rulers of the oases. We know about this from later sources, but may presume the practice had a long history.

Can we assert that the social structures of the Avesta lasted into Achaemenid times? In the Avesta we find the family (*nmana-*) the basis of society, and above the family was the clan (*vis-*), while above the clan was the tribe (*zantu-*). In Persis, after the time of Cyrus, the clan lost its importance and the tribe became subordinate to the government of the province or satrapy, while above the satrapy the nation or state (*khshathra-*) became an important segment of loyalty and identity. In Central Asia, however, we may guess that the old system remained stronger than in the west, and the tribe still wielded influence and power, much greater than in Persis. The formation of a confederacy of tribes in Central Asia did not instill the same allegiance to the confederacy that existed in the kingdoms of Babylonia and Egypt, however, which had ancient traditions upheld by the people. How far loyalty to, and identity with, the Achaemenid Empire prevailed in the east is difficult to determine, but on analogy with later times, loyalty to a leader, in this case the king-of-kings, surely was more important than identification with the institution of emperor and state apparatus. The nomads, of course, were freer in their allegiances than the settled folk.

We have mentioned features of Achaemenid rule applied to the ruling classes, but what were the effects of Achaemenid rule for the common people of Central Asia? Under the Achaemenids the use of iron spread everywhere, and it became commonplace, rather than being limited only to chiefs, leaders or soldiers. The potter's wheel too was in full operation everywhere, undoubtedly aided by imperial centralization, which made communications easier than previously. The increase in settlements, and in land under irrigation, could be attributed to Achaemenid peace and economic growth. The movement of peoples, and the establishment of colonies in Central Asia, must have influenced interchange of ideas and cultures. After the development and spread of horse riding on the steppes of Central Asia by the time of the Achaemenids, the nomadic-settled confrontation was not only a reality, but influenced the settlement patterns, as well as the cooperation of settled folk in common projects directed against nomadic attacks. In short, the Achaemenid period of history promoted the ethnic or individual identity of the peoples of Central Asia (Bactrians, Sogdians, etc.), but it also left a legacy of a great Iranian empire as the center of the world in which all the conquered peoples participated. Just how closely the peoples of Central Asia identified themselves as members of a great Aryan family related to Persians and Medes is unknown. Also their relationship to other subjects of the Achaemenid king—Babylonians, Anatolians, etc.—is difficult to understand, but the contacts made surely influenced thinking and left a legacy for the future.

Another feature of Achaemenid rule, which should be mentioned, was the "law of the king" (*data da malka* in Aramaic), which is known from the Bible, and from loan words in Armenian and other languages of the Near East. We may suppose that the imperial law, which was probably based on Babylonian law codes, and secular in nature, as contrasted with local religious laws of the Hebrews, Egyptians and others, surely was also current in Central Asia. Trained judges probably were sent to Central Asia, as elsewhere, and since the Khwarazmian and Sogdian words for law came from Old Persian *data*, we have an indication of the influence of Achaemenid imperial law in Central Asia.

The overall picture, meager as it is, shows the Achaemenid period of the history of Central Asia to be one of peace and stability, economic development and growth of population. The Sakas were held in check and, if anything, co-opted into the Achaemenid army, as well as maintaining an equilibrium in relations between settled people and pastoral-ists. Trade flourished and Central Asia maintained commercial and cultural contacts with the rest of the empire. It was not an outlying, backward, or even "colonial" part of the Achaemenid Empire, but a rich goal for Alexander and his army.

# Notes

1. Pyankov has many articles in the *Vestnik Drevnei Istorii* and in collected volumes relating to Central Asia. His book on all the sources, bringing together information from his articles, has rested in the Nauka publishing house in Moscow for many years.
2. W.J. Vogelsang, *The Rise and Organisation of the Achaemenid Empire, The Eastern Iranian Evidence* (Leiden: E.J. Brill, 1992), 344 pp., esp. 304–315.
3. It is interesting to see the followers of the son of a "Cimmerian" king in a cuneiform text from Achaemenid times called Saka Ugutum, which very well may be connected with the general ancient designation of invaders from the east in the third millennium B.C.E., viz. the Guti. Cf. Vogelsang, op. cit., 185.
4. For discussions of the Sakas, and references to the sources, see the book of Vogelsang, also F. Altheim and R. Stiehl, *Geschichte Mittelasiens im Altertum* (Berlin: De Gruyter, 1970), 126–30, and my *The History of Ancient Iran* (Munich: C.H. Beck, 1983), 95 and 103, as well as the fundamental work by Julius Junge, *Saka Studien* (Leipzig: Dieterich, 1939), 115 pp.
5. Cf. K.A. Akishev, *Kurgan Issyk* (Moscow, 1978), 47, and V. Sarinidi, *L'or de la Bactriane* (Leningrad: Aurora, 1985); for women cf. graves 2 and 6. (The French translation is better than the English).
6. Rather than giving source references to various Classical and other sources, I refer the reader to the book by Junge, or the chapter "Media" by Igor M. Dyakonov in the *Cambridge History of Iran*, ed. I. Gershevitch (Cambridge: Cambridge University

Press, 1985), 36–149. For a bibliography on the Medes see Bruno Genito, "The Medes: A Reassessment of the Archaeological Evidence," *East and West* 36 (Rome, 1986), 11–81.

7. For a detailed study of the campaign of Cyrus in the east see Igor N. Khlopin, "Baktriiskii pokhod Kira II," *Altorientalische Forschungen I* (Berlin: Akademie Verlag, 1974), 207–16, as well as Dyakonov, loc. cit., and other writings.

8. For a discussion of this migration with references see Altheim and Stiehl, op. cit., 186–190.

9. Many publications on the Aramaic papyri exist; the classical publication is by A. Cowley, *Aramaic Papyri of the Fifth Century B.C.* (Oxford: Clarendon, 1923), 248–71: letter 6, line 2 and letter 8, line 23.

10. Loc. cit., 14–15 and 298–300.

11. The village of Kurkat(h), located near Khojent, should preserve the name, but I suspect that in this case the name was applied to a district, and may have been retained only by this village. Some have assigned the ancient town to modern Ura Tiube.

12. See the basic work by D. Schlumberger, *L'Argent grec dans l'empire achéménide*, Memoirs Délégation Archéologique Française en Afghanistan 14 (Paris, 1953).

13. Cf. M. Griaznov, *L'art ancien d'Altai* (Leningrad, 1958). Many books and articles have been written about this carpet, called the oldest preserved carpet in the world. For a series of articles on Greek influences in Central Asia see I.R. Pichikyan, ed., *Antichnost' i Antichnye traditsii v kulture i iskusstve narodov Sovetsgovo Vostoka* (Moscow, 1978).

14. The Central Asian sources for minerals in this period have been discussed by B. Fleming, "Darius I's Foundation Charters from Susa and the Eastern Achaemenid Empire," *Afghan Studies* 3–4 (1982), 81–87.

# CHAPTER 6

# Alexander and the Heritage of Hellenism

The consequences of Alexander's conquest of the Achaemenid Empire were similar to the recent impact of the West on the rest of the world.[1] For the Near East and Central Asia, however, the Arab conquests and Islam made a still more lasting and penetrating revolution in culture and society. Nonetheless, Hellenism was a powerful force that brought a change in thinking, especially in the realms of culture and, of course, religion, for the peoples of Central Asia. The history of the area was dominated for over a century by the Greco-Bactrian kingdoms and Hellenistic culture, which profoundly changed the face of Central Asia. Let us begin with the conquests of Alexander.

More books have been written about Alexander than any other person in ancient history. The Classical sources have been combed for every detail about his military accomplishments, his purported vision of uniting Greeks and Orientals in one world, and countless other facets of his conquest of the Achaemenid Empire. Here we can be concerned only with his activities in Central Asia and their aftermath. What do we know about his movements in Central Asia?

He crossed the Hindukush Mountains from the south in the spring of 329 B.C.E. in pursuit of Bessus, murderer of Darius Commodanus and satrap of combined Bactria and Sogdiana, who had declared himself the successor of Darius, adopting the throne name Artaxerxes IV. Bessus must have thought that he had a chance of restoring the Iranian part of the Achaemenid Empire, or at least its eastern lands. Although Bessus seems to have been in origin a Persian, he believed that the people of Central Asia would rally to him. The Bactrians, as practical traders and farmers, however, were loath to fight against a powerful newcomer from a distant land, and on the whole they submitted to Alexander,

*Figure 4.* Takht-e Sangin, fragment of ivory carved with head of
Alexander of Macedonia, Seleucid period

especially after witnessing his military prowess and speed in
marches. After some fighting Bessus was captured and later
executed, but resistance did not cease as a result.

To the north of Bactria the Sogdians and Sakas were not
as ready to submit as were the Bactrians, and they offered
strong resistance to the invaders. Alexander, however, was
able to take Samarkand, where he established a garrison,
after which he reached the limits of the Achaemenid Empire
in the east, and reportedly founded a city near or on the site
of modern Khojent.

Another leader had appeared in place of Bessus, a
Sogdian lord called Spitamenes in the Classical sources, and
he secured support from the Sakas. While Alexander was
busy in the Khojent area Spitamenes attacked and defeated
Alexander's garrison near Samarkand. Alexander, in a swift

100

march from the east, drove his opponent into the steppes before retiring to Bactra (also called Zariaspa) for the winter of 329–28 B.C.E. In the early spring Alexander moved north and Spitamenes was forced to flee again. This time his Saka allies apparently decided to make peace and killed Spitamenes, sending his head to Alexander. In the face of such a display of force by Alexander resistance began to crumble, and the last campaign of the Macedonian king was against a Bactrian lord called Oxyartes, who had taken refuge in a strong mountain redoubt, thinking himself safe there. His fortress was taken, but Alexander pardoned the Bactrian and married his daughter the beautiful Roxane. About the same time Apama, daughter of Spitamenes, became the wife of Seleucus I Nikator and the mother of Antiochus I.

Alexander realized that he could not control the vast empire he had conquered with Greek and Macedonian troops alone, so the process of amalgamation of the local population with his garrison troops began. In the beginning, since Persians were the majority of the high officials of the Achaemenid Empire, he had to rely on them to assist him, especially in the Iranian part of the empire. But in Central Asia he found that real power was in the hands of local lords, and he had to enlist their support. While he wintered in Bactra/Balkh, the ruler of Choresmia, called Pharasmanes, had come to him to make peace, and had been reinstated in his domain by Alexander. This apparently happened in a number of cases.

A certain Artabazos had been named satrap of Bactria and Sogdiana after the capture of Bessus, but because of his age he asked to resign and was replaced in 328 B.C.E. by Amyntas, a Macedonian. Because of continued unrest among the local population, it was clear that strong forces of Greeks and Macedonians had to be assigned to Amyntas when Alexander left Central Asia for India in the spring of 327 B.C.E.

The situation in Central Asia after the departure of Alexander can best be characterized as a double rule of the Iranian bureaucracy (including local lords) and the foreigners, who retained control of the army and collection of taxes. A parallel with the later Arab conquests in Central Asia is striking. Many Greeks in the garrisons must have longed for their homelands beside the sea, but several attempts to revolt and return to their distant homelands on the whole were unsuccessful (Curtius IX.7.2).

Much has been written about Alexander's policy of fusion of his followers with the local populations, but in my opinion, attempts to portray Alexander as ahead of his time, in proclaiming a philosophy of universal equality in his "one world" empire, are overblown. As a matter of necessity he had to incorporate local troops into his army, and he had to rely on former Achaemenid officials to govern, but the touchstone was hardly an enlightened view of the world, but rather loyalty to his person, whether Macedonian or Iranian. From the accounts of historians on his campaigns, it is apparent that Alexander only trusted those who were devoted and beholden to him for their positions.

Before his death, however, Greek and Macedonian officers began to replace Iranians in high positions. Whether this ostensible change in policy was the result of pressure by his own officers, or his later disinclination to trust Iranians in positions of power and authority, is not easy to determine. Under the successors of Alexander, however, power remained only in the hands of the Greco-Macedonian aristocracy, who comprised the leaders of the cores of the armies which were formed by the Diadochi, as the rulers were called.

It was quite clear by the time of Alexander, if not previously, that local, popular armies were no match for a well-organized and disciplined professional force. For a long time Greek mercenaries had been the most effective fighting force in the ancient world, and the Macedonians not only united the Greeks under their banner but improved battle tactics. Young Iranians were organized by Alexander into a special bodyguard on the Macedonian model, and many local levies were incorporated into his army, but garrisons, mostly composed of Greeks, were left in various centers of the east. These constituted pockets of power under local Greek or Macedonian officers, but whether the forces under them were solely Greco-Macedonian, or also comprised local soldiers, is uncertain. Alexander seems to have feared that local, mercenary armies might contest central authority, for in 324 B.C.E. he ordered all such forces to be disbanded, but before this could happen he died in Babylon in 323 B.C.E. (Arrian VII.6.1 foll.).

The legacy left by Alexander was far-reaching. Stories and romances about him existed in many languages of the east, and he assumed superhuman dimensions in most of them.[2] In the Iranian world Alexander was either co-opted or anathematized. In the first case, Alexander was declared really to have been the son of an Achaemenid prince who had taken refuge in Macedonia and married the mother of Alexander, while in the latter case the Middle Persian book *Arda Viraf Namak* gives the view of the later Zoroastrian religious establishment when it describes him as "that wicked, miserable, heretic, sinful, hateful Alexander the Roman, resident of Egypt."[3] Both views of Alexander were current also in Central Asia, and it is impossible to disentangle them, except to say that later Christian missionaries, among others, propagated a favorable impression of Alexander wherever they went in the east. This was the prevailing view of Alexander in Islamic times as well.

More important were the consequences of the establishment of garrisons, and the building of Greek towns in the east, most of which, however, were the result of Seleucid policy rather than Alexander's own achievement. What was the situation in Central Asia at the death of Alexander?

In Parthia and Hyrcania an Iranian, Phrataphernes, remained as satrap until his death in 321 B.C.E., when he was followed by Philip, presumably a Macedonian. Arsaces, or Arsames, satrap of Areia (Herat), was replaced by Stasanor after the death of Alexander. Oxyartes, Alexander's father-in-law, had been named satrap of the Hindukush region, but apparently resigned after a short tenure. We do not hear of his replacement by a Greek or Macedonian, and may presume that local chiefs maintained their authority in the mountains. Bactria and Sogdiana apparently were under Philip until Antipater became the next regent of Alexander's domains after the assassination of Perdikkas, Alexander's successor, in 321 B.C.E. Stasanor was then sent to Bactria by Antipater, and a Cypriote called Stasander became satrap of Herat and Sistan (Diodorus XVIII.39.6).

It almost seems that a game of musical chairs was played by Alexander's officers in the eastern part of his former empire. At first the eastern satraps were appointed by the central authority, but they soon showed such independence that various generals seeking Alexander's position, especially Antigonos, the most successful, had to conciliate the satraps to secure their cooperation. Stasanor held his place in Bactria, but Stasander was replaced by Evitus followed by Evagoras. This uncertainty of tenure changed with the conquests of Seleucus in the east (Diodorus XIX.92.5 and Appian, *Syriake,* fragment 55).

We know nothing about the success of Seleucus in the east, except his treaty with Chandragupta Maurya, who secured rule over lands to the south and east of the Hindukush range in exchange for 500 elephants, which helped Seleucus in his victory over Antigonos in 301 B.C.E. (Strabo XV.724). After Seleucus secured the eastern part of his future empire, we no longer find in the sources the name of any of his satraps in the east.

Seleucus and his son Antiochus, by the daughter of Spitamenes, promoted the migration of Greeks and Macedonians to the east, and established Greek towns. Not only Greeks and Macedonians, but also Anatolians, Thracians, and surely others, went to the east (Diodorus XIX.27). It is clear that the Seleucids intended to colonize the east and not simply establish garrisons. Unfortunately we have little information about Central Asia under the early Seleucids, and can only guess at events from brief notices in Classical sources. A certain Demodamas was sent to Central Asia and went as far as the Jaxartes River, after which he wrote a treatise about Central Asia that has not been preserved. Whether he was leading a military expedition or simply exploring is uncertain, but possible threats of nomads from across the river may have been a reason for his journey.

Antiochus was made viceroy of the east by his father

Seleucus ca. 294–93 B.C.E., and probably resided for a time in Bactra as his headquarters. He is said to have built a long wall around the oasis of Merv, where he established a town called Antiochia after his own name (Strabo IX.516 and Pliny VI.47). Probably under his reign the Greek town today called Ay Khanum, on the Oxus and Kokcha rivers in northern Afghanistan, was settled, although it may have been established first by Alexander. Excavations at this site have revealed a pure Greek *polis* with gymnasium, theater and other regular features of a Greek city. From inscriptions we learn that an uncontaminated Greek language was in use in the town, and all the accouterments of Greek culture were present.

The division of authority between the Greek polis, with its civic institutions, and the central government of the Seleucids eludes us, but probably a compromise was reached by which the Greeks of Bactria had more freedom and power than their counterparts in Mesopotamia and Syria, with the two capitals of Seleucia on the Tigris and Antioch on the Orontes.

The discoveries at Ay Khanum and other minor sites in Central Asia have opened new vistas on the extent of Hellenization in the east. For centuries the Greek presence in Bactria was known only by the superb coins of the later Greek kingdom and scattered works of art. Now we know that the Greeks in the east may be compared with the colonizers of Sicily and the northern coasts of the Black Sea, and we may designate the Greek kingdom in the east as one of the successor kingdoms to Alexander, such as those of the Seleucids and Ptolemies. Even when Alexander was alive some garrisons in the east wanted to return home, but under the Seleucids colonists came to Bactria. Were they sent by order of the king, or were they rewarded with land and other inducements to settle far from their homes? Probably both reasons applied, but we hear of no revolts among them against the Seleucids, so one may suppose they mostly came willingly for rewards. In the sources the Seleucid colonists were called *katoikoi,* and received land grants *(kleroi),* for which they had to serve in the army on demand.[4]

Most of the towns established in the east apparently did not have the full-fledged status of a Greek polis, but were a stage below, and the term used for these settlements in the sources is *politeuma*, or we also find *katoikia,* with the inhabitants called by that name as well. Presumably the settlements in the east had a royal *epistates,* or mayor, appointed by the government, at least in the early years of the Seleucid state, whereas later local authority prevailed. We do not know the powers or authority vested in the office, or relations to other officials, but the bureaucracy obviously was more developed and expanded in the Seleucid settlements compared to the pre-Alexander days.

The Greeks used their language as a basis of their administration, and the minting of coins indicates economic prosperity, not only in Bactria but of all the lands under Greek rule in the east. Even in the lands south of the Hindukush, ceded by Seleucus to the Indians, Greek was one of the languages inscribed by Asoka, successor to Chandragupta, on his rock edicts located there. It is fascinating to read the inscriptions, with both Aramaic and Greek translations of the Buddhist edicts.

Presumably relations between the colonists and the local population were much closer than, for example, between the Ptolemaic rulers of Egypt and their subjects. In Bactria, however, Greek replaced the Aramaic of the Achaemenid chancellery as the new bureaucratic language of rule. In passing, it may be mentioned that the Seleucids sent regular embassies to the Indian court, and one of the ambassadors, Megasthenes, wrote a book about his trip there which has survived only in fragments in later authors. In short, under the early Seleucids Hellenic civilization came into contact with local cultures and spread in the east, more in Central Asia than in Iran. Again strikingly, this was similar to the situation later under the Arabs.

When Seleucus died in 281 B.C.E. he was succeeded by Antiochus who inherited many problems in the western part of the empire. For twenty years, until his death in 261 B.C.E., Antiochus was occupied by struggles with the Ptolemies and others; Central Asia went its own way. Yet it still remained loyal to the Seleucid dynasty until it was clear that ties between Bactria and the Mediterranean could not be maintained, especially because of nomad invasions, in particular by the Parni who took over the satrapy of Parthia and Hyrcania from the Seleucid satrap Andragoras. This may have happened in 247 B.C.E., which is the beginning of the Parthian era of time dating, or the dating may represent the crowning of Arsaces, the first Parthian ruler.

It is apparent that the trade route from Mesopotamia to Bactria was the vital link which had to be maintained by the Greeks, since other parts of the Iranian plateau, such as Fars and Azerbaijan, did not receive garrisons or colonists as did Bactria. They were off the road, so to speak, and held to their own dynasts and culture. Central Asia, however, became an outpost of Hellenism, which in the century after the end of effective Seleucid rule in the east had profound influence not only in India but all over Central Asia. The expanded use of coinage indicates a great expansion of economic activity, and surely the prosperity of Central Asia under Seleucid rule caused the population, both native and foreign, to support Seleucid rule. But the Seleucid kings were interested in the west, and all of the east was neglected, which led the Greeks in Central Asia to strike out on their own.

# Notes

1. It is difficult to choose among the plethora of writings about Alexander, even while concentrating on Central Asia. For an extensive bibliography see J. Seibert, *Alexander der Grosse* (Darmstadt: Wissenschaftliche Buchgesellschaft, 1972) and more recently D.J. Ross, *Alexander historiatus* (Frankfurt am Main: Athenäum, 1988).
2. Alexander romances exist in languages ranging from those of Europe to Mongolian. Cf. M. Southgate, *Iskandarnamah, a Persian Medieval Alexander-romance* (New York: Columbia Univ. Press, 1978) and A. Wolohojian, *The Romance of Alexander the Great*, Armenian version (New York: Columbia Univ. Press, 1964).
3. For the *Arda Viraf Namak* cf. F. Vahman, *Arda Wiraz Namag* (Copenhagen, 1986), 191 and 224.

4. The classic work on the organization of the Seleucid state is E. Bikerman, *Institutions des Séleucides* (Paris: Geuthner, 1938), and the most complete study of the eastern provinces may be found in S. Sherwin-Williams and E. Kuhrt, *From Samarkand to Sardis* (Berkeley: Univ. of California Press, 1993).

# CHAPTER 7

# Greco-Bactrians and Parthians

It is interesting that the end of Seleucid authority in the east came from two different peoples and societies: the nomadic Parni and the settled Greeks of Bactria. The former were the first to challenge the Seleucids in Khurasan, and we can reconstruct probable events leading to the rise of the Parthians from the few fragments in Classical sources. Fortunately we have the extensive writings and research of Josef Wolski, who devoted his life to early Parthian history.[1] Although some uncertainty exists, and there are controversies about the origins of the Parthian state, there is now a general consensus about the early history. According to Strabo (XIX.515), the Parni or Aparni were a tribe of the Dahi nomads who lived in Dahistan to the east of the Caspian. Sometime in the first half of the third century B.C.E. the Parni moved south into Seleucid domains in the former Achaemenid satrapy of Parthia. It seems they raided the settled regions many times before they decided to permanently occupy the area. Whether their first capital was Nisa, to the west of present Ashkabad, where extensive excavations have revealed an important Parthian center, is uncertain. Later they moved south and occupied Astauene, present Quchan, in Iran. They attacked and killed the Seleucid governor of Parthia about 250 or 247 B.C.E., according to Justin (XLI.4), but it seems they did not immediately consolidate their power over Parthia after that event, for the campaign of Antiochus III to the east in 209 B.C.E. found the nomadic power ready to acknowledge Seleucid overlordship. Like many nomads in that part of the world, the Parni adopted the language of the settled people, and were absorbed. Hence, the term "Parthians" meant those peoples in the northern part of the Iranian plateau who were subjects of, and used the official written language of, the state, which was formed by

111

*Figure 5.* Parthian hieratic style ivory carving, Hermitage Museum

the first ruler whom we know, called Arshak or Arsaces. This name, like that of Caesar among the Romans, was used by succeeding rulers as their title, as shown on their coins. Because of this, one must rely on styles of the coins, including busts of the ruler, their head-dresses, and other details, to identify which Parthian ruler is represented. Naturally this causes problems and disputes in identifications.

After the defeat of Antio-chus III by the Romans at the battle of Magnesia in 190, the Parthian state expanded west-ward against the Seleucids. The Parthians retained their home-land in present day Turk-menistan, including the oasis of Merv, which they apparently conquered from the Greco-Bactrians, but their capitals moved west with their con-quests. In the east their main energies of later expansion were directed towards India rather than Central Asia, as we shall see. Let us first turn to the Greco-Bactrian kingdom.

The Greco-Bactrians were the heirs of the Achaemenids and Seleucids in Central Asia.[2] It is fascinating to see a pow-erful influence by Greek and Macedonian colonists, who can-not have been great in numbers, exerted in many fields on Central Asia. The most visible, of course, is the heritage of Greek art and architecture, evident from archaeological remains. Perhaps the best parallel to the Greek settlement in Bactria would be the British in India in the 19th century. Yet the site of Ay Khanum, in both its layout and objects excavated there, was a completely Hellenistic city, unlike New Delhi which could not be called an English city. From Greek inscriptions in Ay Khanum, we find both purely Greek names and local, Iranian names, an indication that the local population lived side by side with the Hellenic settlers. Greek culture must have made a deep impression on the local people, more than on the Iranian peoples of the plateau, since so far no comparable site has been found in Iran. It is true that the Parthians too accepted Greek culture, but obviously not so wholeheartedly as in the east. One reason probably was the concentration of Greek colonists in Bactria, key for routes to Central Asia and India, even more than in sites on the long road from Mesopotamia to the east, although archaeologists have not yet had a chance to excavate Hellenistic towns in Iran. But both in Azerbaijan and in Fars province the Greek presence seemingly was negligible in comparison to the main route to the east. Ay Khanum was not unique, however, for other settlements such as those in Kandahar, in Ghazni (Alexandria in Arachosia ?), in Kapisa or Begram (Alexandria ad Caucasum), guarded routes of trade going to India, probably following Achaemenid forerunners. The colonists sent to Bactria surely were no different from those in the western part of the Seleucid domains, but local conditions may have influenced the number and type of colonists, not only for strategic reasons, but also because of the need to hold together to oversee water for irrigation, and other factors in the east.

Seleucid possessions south of the Hindukush Mountains, which had been ceded by Seleucus I to Chandragupta Maurya, never returned to Seleucid rule, not even after the expedition of Antiochus III, but Greeks continued to live in southern towns under the rule of the Mauryas. In the north, however, colonists, especially from Asia Minor, were continually encouraged to settle in Bactria, and not only were towns built, but agriculture flourished under expanded irrigation, and the area became rich. Originally the Bactrian kingdom was the center of a large area, which included Sogdiana, the Merv oasis, and Herat in the southwest, but as settlements

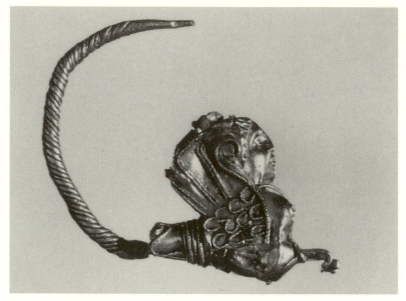

*Figure 6.* Dushanbe, gold pendant in form of a sphinx, Kushan period

increased in Sogdiana, this region became separate and probably about 170 B.C.E. it became virtually independent under local rulers. Merv, as noted, at some time was lost to the Parthians.

With the attention of the Seleucids ever more turned towards the west, Diodotus, satrap of the vast Bactrian region, declared his independence from the Seleucids, probably tentatively after the death of Antiochus II in 246 B.C.E., but openly several years later. It is uncertain whether the issuance of coins in his own name really meant complete independence from the Seleucids, for the trade routes to the west were not broken. It seems that the economic self-sufficiency of Bactria was an important factor in the loosening of ties with the Seleucid west.

It is unknown how far the Greeks in Bactria followed the Seleucid practice of a cult dedicated to the dead ruler, and then to the living ruler or his spouse from the time of Antiochus III. There is no evidence that the cult of the king, dead or living, was an important factor either in the lives of the Greek colonists or among the native population, although it is possible. Other matters probably had a greater priority in the concerns of the Greco-Bactrians. At all times there was the threat of nomadic invasion from the north, and the Greco-Bactrian kingdom had to guard against such incursions. But the wealth of the land, as well as commerce, gave the new kingdom the means not only to maintain its power but to expand into India.

Diodotus I was followed by his son Diodotus II, and then by a certain Euthydemus I, who is said to have assassinated his predecessor (Polybius XI.34). Under these three kings (ca. 246–205 B.C.E.) rule was limited to Bactria and its northern provinces, but afterwards the riches of the south lured rulers to conquests there. Euthydemus may have made forays to the south but his son Demetrius I is a more likely candidate for raids if not conquests in India. Whether he conquered the Kabul valley, and as far as Arachosia, however, is uncertain, for a find spot of coins does not necessarily indicate occupation by a certain ruler, whose coins are found there. A reconstruction of history based solely on numismatics can be misleading and we are reduced to guesses.

The history of the Greco-Bactrian kingdom is based overwhelmingly on coinage since the literary references are very few. The coins are beautiful examples of Greek monetary art, with distinctive features of the kings finely portrayed on the obverses of the coins. By analysis of facial features, symbols, weights and find spots, numismatists have been able to bring order into the plethora of coins minted by the Greco-Bactrian rulers.

Demetrius, the son of Euthydemus, probably crossed the Hindukush, but the extent of his conquests remains conjectural. From finds of coins, however, one may suggest that Greco-Bactrian domains under the successors of Demetrius extended to present southern Afghanistan and part of Sistan, as well as northwest India. How long and under which rulers various regions remained under Greek rule is difficult to determine. According to Justin (XLI.6) a certain Eucratides seized power about 171 B.C.E. and ruled until 145, making conquests in India, but according to Strabo (XI.517) he lost land to the Parthians in the west, which was probably Areia and neighboring territory. Afterwards the coinage shows many rulers, and we are reduced only to conjectures.

From the coinage, one might propose that the Greco-Bactrian kingdom divided, since numismatists find coins of rulers whom they designate as successors of Eucratides primarily north of the Hindukush, while those of successors of the family of Euthydemus and Demetrius are concentrated south of the mountains. But even this surmise has exceptions.[3] Generally speaking, coins based on the Attic standard, and with Greek legends alone, are thought to have been struck north of the Hindukush, while those with bilingual (Prakrit in the Kharoshthi alphabet and Greek) legends and Indian weight standards are assigned to the Indian borderlands. Many rulers, however, coined both types, and it is difficult to place them in time or space.[4]

A famous Greek ruler called Menander (ca. 150–135 B.C.E.) made extensive conquests in India, and his name has come down in Buddhist sources as a patron of that religion. The number of various coins of Greek rulers in India and southern Afghanistan may indicate a shifting of Greco-Bactrian power and interest into India, leaving the lands to the north of the Hindukush in the hands of local satraps or lords. Imitations of Greco-Bactrian coins, struck by local rulers in the north, complicate the picture of political rule. Since we are not concerned with the Greeks in India we should ask what did happen north of the Hindukush after the death of Eucratides?

Numismatists suggest that Heliocles was the last Greek king to rule a central kingdom on the plains of Bactria, from ca. 145 to 130 B.C.E., although the coins of Hermaeus imply that he ruled much later somewhere in the Hindukush Mountains, possibly as a vassal of the Kushans. Another ruler, Antimachus, whose coins have been found in Central Asia, also may have ruled a mountain domain north of the Hindukush after the invasion of nomads, while it cannot be excluded that other petty rulers continued to exist and strike coins. By the time of the establishment of the Kushan Empire in the first century C.E., however, coins with Greek names on them such as Archebios and Hippostratus are considered to be restricted to India.

From Chinese and Greek sources we may reconstruct the scenario of the end of Greek rule in Bactria, when Greek possessions south of the mountains had to contend not only with bands of Central Asian nomads, but also later with Parthian expansion. Before turning to the momentous events which changed the history of Central Asia, a brief return glance at the Parthians may be in order.

Mithradates I (ca. 171–138 B.C.E.) is the first Parthian ruler whose coins are abundant and found in many sites, indicating a consolidation of power and the formation of a state on the Iranian plateau. Although we have no information, it is possible that it was this Mithradates who took lands in the general region of Herat from the Greco-Bactrians. But after his death the Parthians, like the Greco-Bactrians, suffered from the invasion of nomads from Central Asia. Phraates, successor of Mithradates, was defeated and killed by the Sakas, one of the peoples in the invasion. His uncle and successor Artabanus was also killed fighting the nomads in 123 B.C.E., and it was not until the reign of Mithradates II (ca. 123–87 B.C.E.) that Parthian power again was felt in the east. Probably the Sakas who settled in Sistan (Sakastan), recognized his authority and became vassals of Mithradates. Later, as one may infer from the Parthian names on coins of rulers in southern Afghanistan and India—Vonones, Spalahores, Spalirises, and Gondophares—Parthian princes ruled over the local populations, including Sakas. But that is not part of the history of Central Asia.

## Notes

1. A general summary of Jozef Wolski's theories appears in his book *L'Empire des Arsacides,* Acta Iranica 32 (Louvain: Peeters, 1993), 218 pp. For a bibliography of his many writings (with much repetition) see E. Dabrowa, "Bibliografia 1937–1979," in *Zeszyty naukowe uniwersytetu Jagiellonskiego,* prace historyczne z. 70 (Cracow, 1981). For general works see M. Colledge, *The Parthians* (London, 1967), and G. Koshelenko, *Rodina*

*Parfyan* (Moscow, 1977).

2. The two basic books on the Greco-Bactrians, which should be used with caution, however, are W. Tarn, *The Greeks in Bactria and India* (Cambridge: Cambridge Univ. Press, 1951) and A. Narain, *The Indo-Greeks* (Oxford, 1957). Since then many articles by numismatists have added to our knowledge of the Greco-Bactrians.
3. Cf. Tarn, op. cit., 222–24.
4. The most recent survey of the coinage is by O. Bopearachichi, *Monnaies gréco-bactriennes et indo-grecques. Catalogue raisonné* (Paris: Bibliothèque Natl., 1991)

# CHAPTER 8

# Nomadic Interlude

The changes wrought in Central Asia at the end of the second century B.C.E. were caused not only by the weakness of the Greco-Bactrian domains, or by internecine strife, but also by the size and intensity of the nomadic invasions of that period.[1] Previously there had been raids by nomads, and even a movement of the Parni into Parthia, but the magnitude and variety of tribes in the new movement of peoples may be compared to the *Völkerwanderung* of the Germanic tribes at the end of the Roman Empire.

If we can rely on Chinese sources, the movement of the tribes began on the frontiers of China in what today is the province of Gansu. From archaeology, including mummies found in the Taklamakan desert, the ancient inhabitants of the western regions of China were Europoids rather than Mongolian in physical appearance. We cannot assume, however, that they were originally speakers of Indo-European languages, for these aborigines may have existed there from very ancient times. The curtain of history is raised on them in the second century B.C.E., when they were attacked by another and presumably different group of nomads from the north, called Hiung-nu or Hsiung-nu by the Chinese sources.

Undoubtedly there had been clashes between the Chinese and their northern neighbors from ancient times, but in the time of the Chou dynasty (until the 3d century B.C.E.), the power of the feudal lords and the lack of unity among the nomadic tribes seems to have maintained a balance of power between the nomads and the settled populations. It is not until the time of the "Warring States" period of Chinese history, when a number of kingdoms were formed, three of whom faced the northern nomads—the Ch'in, Chao and Yen—that some control over the inroads of the northerners appears. They all began to build walls against the raids of the nomads, but only when China was unified by the first emperor of the Ch'in dynasty in 221 B.C.E. were the walls joined to make the "Great Wall" against the nomads. The Ch'in empire was replaced by an even more powerful dynasty, that of the Han, in 202 B.C.E. At the same time the Hiung-nu were united, and soon a nomadic empire faced the Chinese in conflict; this opposition, now between a settled empire and a nomadic empire, continued for centuries.

The Hiung-nu also attacked the non-Chinese tribes of the Gansu corridor, called Yüeh-chih in Chinese sources. After several defeats the latter broke into two parts, the Small Yüeh-chih and the Large Yüeh-chih. The former moved south into the mountainous area occupied by Tibetan peoples, while the larger band moved westward about 175 B.C.E., through Dzungaria to the fertile Ili valley. Some twelve years later the Hiung-nu, together with a vassal tribe called Wu-sun in Chinese sources, attacked the Large Yüeh-chih and drove them from the Ili valley, which was then occupied by the Wu-sun. The Yüeh-chih moved south into western Central Asia, and they forced other nomads to move or flee before them even farther south. The Hiung-nu established a hegemony over the oasis states of the Tarim basin, whose inhabitants were no longer identified as Yüeh-chih or other peoples in the Chinese writings, but simply as *Hu,* "barbarians."

The Yüeh-chih problem has produced an enormous literature, as mentioned above, because it is not only an historical problem of identification of these people, but also a linguistic matter, since they have been identified as speakers of two dialects of the *centum* Tokharian language, whose descendants wrote texts in that language found in Kucha and elsewhere in the northern Tarim basin. Reconstruction of the ancient pronunciation of the Chinese characters has produced many theories about the identification of the Tokharians, with no consensus. However, it is now generally accepted that the Tokharians were one tribe of the confederation of the Yüeh-chih who eventually founded the Kushan Empire, and gave their name to medieval Tokharistan, ancient Bactria and present Badakhshan. Presumably some of the confederation remained in the oases of the northern

Tarim, and their descendants produced writings in the language generally called Tokharian by modern scholars.

The Altaic speaking Hiung-nu did not enter western Central Asia at this time, and by the first century of our era several divisions had occurred in their realm, for instance the division between the northern Hiung-nu, beyond Chinese control, and the southern group which had submitted to Chinese hegemony. One divisive factor among the Hiung-nu was the order of succession, which usually made the younger brother of the ruler, instead of his son, his successor. This caused much disorder and rebellion at the death of a leader. During this period, however, first western Mongolia, then the Ili valley and adjacent areas were being infiltrated by Altaic speakers, who mingled with the Iranian speaking peoples and others in these regions. The "others" may have been Uralic speakers or groups now long extinct.

The political picture of Central Asia about the year 150 B.C.E. may be described as follows: In China proper the Han dynasty had replaced the Ch'in, and peace had been made with the Hiung-nu in 198 B.C.E., by which the Chinese had recognized Hiung-nu rule over the lands beyond the Great Wall, including the oasis states of the west. Many gifts were sent yearly by the Han court to the Hiung-nu chief Motun, and peace was maintained, in spite of some raids by the successors of Motun after his death in 174 B.C.E. In the Ili valley and the western steppes of present Kazakhstan lived the Wu-sun, vassals of the Hiung-nu. They may have been the ancestors of the As, a branch of the later Alans, all Iranian speakers. To the south, the Yüeh-chih had conquered the kingdom of K'ang-chü, located in the area of present Tashkent, and also some of Sogdiana. More likely, one should say that they had established an hegemony over the settled people of the oases, for confederation was the means of creating an empire for nomads, and they had not yet created an empire which included settled populations, according to the Chinese.

In 150 B.C.E. the Greco-Bactrians probably still ruled the land to the south of the Hissar mountains, under Eucratides. The western bank of the Oxus River also may have been part of Greco-Bactrian domains, or ruled by a local Sogdian lord, or even under Parthian rule. For the Parthians at this time seem to have ruled both Merv and Herat, as well as their own lands to the west. There is no evidence for petty rulers related to the Parthians in any eastern region, including India, at this time. To the south of the Hindukush Mountains were other Greek rulers, including Menander, but what their relations with Eucratides, or among themselves, were we can only guess.

The fusion of Greeks with local populations was well under way, and the Greeks had long espoused the worship of Central Asian divinities, or had identified them with their own. This is clear from the temples in Ay Khanum, or in a temple site on the Oxus today called Takht-e Sangin, dedicated to local deities, while the process of syncretism had progressed as it had in the west. On the coins, however, Hellenistic appellatives such as *soter,* "savior," continued in use, indicating the strength of Hellenic culture beyond the fall of the Greek kingdoms. Presumably the governmental organizations of the Bactrian state continued to function, but much of the military strength had been shifted to India.

There is an enigma regarding the position of the Sakas at about 150 B.C.E. They are presumed to have been the most numerous of the nomads living around the oases of Central Asia. Later we find Saka kingdoms established in ancient Drangiana, present Sistan, which took its name from the Sakas, and in southern Afghanistan and India, as well as in the oasis of Khotan in eastern Turkestan. When did the Sakas move into these areas?

From Justin (XLII) and Strabo (XI.8) we learn that a confederation of tribes ended Greek rule in Bactria about 130 B.C.E., where it seems Heliocles, successor of Eucratides, was ruling. Usually, in the conquests by nomadic hordes, either the enemy tribes were driven in flight from the conquerors, or they were incorporated into the confederation. It seems that primarily the latter was the case in the fall of the Greco-Bactrian kingdom, but then many Sakas moved south to Sistan and on to India while other nomads remained in Sogdiana and Bactria.

From literary remains of what we call the Khotan-Saka language, so named because the language is essentially the same as that on inscriptions and coins of the Saka rulers in India, we can only speculate on the origin of the Saka occupation of the southern oases in eastern Turkestan. Presumably they occupied the oases of Kashgar, Yarkand, and Khotan, as well as smaller settlements to the east. One suggestion is that the Saka domination was a slow process, perhaps absorbing the ancestors of the Burushaski inhabitants of present Hunza, as well as Indian trading colonies, attested by the discovery of Prakrit fragments, older than the Khotanese-Saka literary remains. This presumes a Saka infiltration into the east even before the Achaemenid Empire, which is not unlikely. By the time of the Greco-Bactrians these Sakas should have been in place in the east. It is also possible that some Saka bands went over the high mountains from eastern Turkestan to the plains of India at the end of the second century B.C.E., but this is uncertain.

The nomads succeeded in wresting political control of Central Asia from the settled folk, so that in 100 B.C.E. we see a different picture of kingdoms in the east. This is the period of rule of the Parthian king Mithradates II (ca. 123–87 B.C.E.). The Sakas had occupied Sistan and had defeated two Parthian kings, who lost their lives in battle, but Mithradates II, who took the title "king of kings," implying conquest over minor rulers, restored Parthian authority in the east. Whether the Saka chiefs who were settled in Sistan became vassals of the Parthians or accepted Parthian hegemony in some fashion is unclear. Presumably trade routes were either maintained or re-established with India for the next century and more. The year 100 B.C.E. sees the beginning of a mixture of Saka and Parthian local rulers in Sistan, southern Afghanistan and the northwest of the Indian subcontinent.

It is now generally agreed that one tribe of the Yüeh-chih of Chinese sources laid the foundation for the state which succeeded the Greek kingdom of Bactria, and which became known after the name of that tribe as the Kushan Empire. In Indian sources the Yavanas (Greeks), Pahlavas (Parthians) and Sakas are usually mentioned together as peoples and rulers of the northwest of the subcontinent, and as predecessors of the Kushans. The sequence of rulers in Afghanistan and the northwest subcontinent, is determined from legends and styles of their coinage, as well as overstrikes of the coins of one ruler by another. From the coinage, and especially the names of rulers on the coins, it seems that Saka, Greek and Parthian petty rulers reigned simultaneously in different areas, so that the period from the death of Mithradates II to the reign of Vima Kadphises, who was the Kushan king about 60 C.E., may be characterized as an era of various small principalities, while the Kushans were slowly consolidating their power north of the Hindukush Mountains.

It is not the purpose of this book to discuss details such as the possible sequences of rulers in various regions, but to present a general assessment of the changes in the history of Central Asia from an overall point of view. The aftermath of the fall of the Greco-Bactrian kingdom was an age of nomadic invasion and rule in Central Asia. Undoubtedly changes occurred in the administration of conquered territories, but how much of the existing bureaucracy and society continued under the new rulers? We should remember that just as the Achaemenid administration had continued under the Seleucids, with a Hellenic addition, so the Greco-Bactrian state must have served as a model for the nomads. But in the Bactrian heartland Seleucid institutions had held sway, to such an extent that Greek really replaced Aramaic as the only language of administration. In Sogdiana and the Parthian lands of present Turkmenistan, however, Aramaic remained the primary administrative tongue until the first centuries of our era, when local languages, written in varieties of the Aramaic script, replaced the imperial Aramaic of Achaemenid times. South of the Hindukush Mountains, however, Indian influences prevailed, including the use of first Kharoshthi, and then Brahmi scripts. What was the situation to the east of the Pamirs at this time?

By 100 B.C.E. the peace between the Han Empire and the Hiung-nu had long since ended, and the Chinese were in the ascendancy in the oasis states of the Tarim basin. After the dispatch of an ambassador Chang Ch'ien by the Han ruler Wu-ti to the Yüeh-chih, who returned in 126 B.C.E. and wrote a report of his travels, Chinese communications were opened with the Ferghana valley and other regions of western Central Asia. According to the *Shih-chi* (ch. 123), the important Chinese historical work of this period, in 101 B.C.E. a Chinese general called Li Kuang-li was able to besiege the chief city of Ferghana and secure its submission. So Chinese power and influence was felt for the first time in the far west of China. From this time events in Mongolia, China and east Turkestan influenced many regions of Central Asia including the western part. From their later locations, we may assume that various tribes of nomads, both large and small, moved from one part of Central Asia to another, the records of which do not exist. Much of our conjecture depends on the appearance and disappearance of names of nomads in Chinese sources, and for them events in the far west may be based more on rumors than on factual information.

The oasis states of both eastern and western Central Asia had similar histories of invasion and domination by nomadic tribes from the north, but the eastern oases also had to contend with Chinese attempts to control them. A diplomatic game of playing the Chinese against the northern nomads became the hallmark of politics in Central Asia, especially by the states of the northern Tarim basin. The Chinese, of course, were experts on *divide et impera,* and used various factions in the oases for their own purposes.

For over three centuries western Central Asia had been under foreign domination, first the Achaemenids and then the Greeks. But neither power had imposed a heavy yoke on the people of the region. The new, and presumably larger, group of nomadic invaders were content to accept the civilization they found and to adapt their own traditions to it somewhat. It is likely that the Greco-Bactrians lost the territories north of the Hissar Mountain range several decades before the invasion of their central lands south of the mountains about 130 B.C.E. The tribes of the nomadic confederation which invaded Bactria were called by Classical authors the Asii, Tokhari and Sakarauli or Saraucae, with many vari-

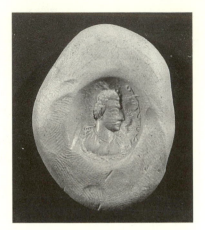

*Figure 7.* A seal impression of a
Hephthalite princess (?) with a
defective inscription.

*Figure 8.* A seal impression
of a Hephthalite prince
reading dezono (?)

ants. The last named should be the Sakas, or a certain tribe
of them. The others are the Yüeh-chih of the Chinese, but
obviously on their way to the Oxus River they picked up other tribes. It is possible that the Asii were a tribe of those later called Alans, and that a variant reading for one of the
invaders, Pasiani, conceivably could be the ancestors of the
Pashtuns, but this is mere speculation. What is clear is that
there was a massive invasion of the Greco-Bactrian kingdom,
and that some Sakas probably stayed in Bactria while others
went south to Sistan and to India. Other tribes remained
north of the Oxus, according to Chinese sources, and only
moved across the river into Bactria more than a century later. These would be the tribes associated with the Kushans.
But for more than a century after the fall of the Greco-
Bactrian kingdom in Bactria, we are in the dark about the
situation in western Central Asia. It is impossible to assign
definite territories of rule to the tribes, and all we can say is
that for the century and a half from 130 B.C.E. to ca. 20 C.E.,
Central Asia was dominated by various nomadic tribes, possibly in joint rule with local Greco-Bactrian potentates.

As previously mentioned, in the area of Tashkent the
account of Chang Ch'ien, ambassador of the Han court, tells

of a kingdom called K'ang-chü, while later, merchants and others coming to China from Samarkand are called people of K'ang. This may mean a union of the two countries at some time, but what is significant is the Chinese description of both K'ang-chü and Ferghana as dominated by nomads. Perhaps this means a return to pastoralism of many people in the two regions, for previously there had been towns in both areas. On the other hand, at this time it seems that they were not as heavily populated as areas to the south. Probably urbanization was not dominant in either the Ferghana valley or the Tashkent plain, and it was easy for nomads to cover the countryside.

Obviously the Yüeh-chih represented an important horde in the eyes of the Chinese, who would not have sent an envoy so far to seek their alliance against the Hiung-nu, which never materialized. In Xinjiang the oasis states had come under Chinese authority, since the Hiung-nu power had declined through inner conflicts. By the end of the long reign of the Han emperor Wu-ti (ca. 140–87 B.C.E.) China was at the peak of its power and influence in Central Asia, and even distant Ferghana had made peace with a Chinese army sent against it. The Hiung-nu lost the dominant position they held in the north of the Tarim basin, but Chinese fortunes went up and down in the region, with local revolts against their authority, whenever the Chinese had to retreat because of their own internal problems.

The nomadic interlude in the west produced no great changes among the settled populations, who greatly influenced their overlords with their culture. At the same time, the nomads long maintained their own way of life, and brought new styles into the amalgam of art and culture which was being created in Bactria.

The cultural situation in Bactria is well illustrated by finds in nomadic graves, especially Tilla Tepe in northern Afghanistar., dating probably from the first century, where many objects in gold were found.[2] Among the objects such as belt buckles, jewelry of various kinds, and plaques, we find the Greek realistic style, a nomadic style of imaginary, twisted animals, either hunter and hunted or in combat, a hieratic "Parthian" style, and even influences from India. This manifold culture is characteristic of the nomadic age before the consolidation of the Kushan Empire. It was characteristic of a time of change.

The same profusion of artistic styles is paralleled by the religious situation, where various deities are worshipped, and it continues into the Kushan period, where it is particularly evident on the coinage. It is impossible to determine whether certain divinities were only honored in particular places, or by certain tribes, or whether the pantheon was widespread and universally worshipped. But the identification of Greek gods and goddesses with Iranian and Indian deities parallels the same kind of process in the Near East during the Hellenistic age. Furthermore, sacrifices or dedications to the spirits or deities of particular places, such as the Oxus River at the temple at Takht-e Sangin, are attested. Cults of ancestors probably existed among both the settled and nomadic peoples. The nomads, we suppose, brought their own shamanistic beliefs and practices to the settled population, adding to the amalgam. At no time, however, do we find a large, well organized or hierarchical priesthood of a cult or sect similar to the priesthood of the Zoroastrian church under the Sasanians. This era, of course, predated the spread of the universal religions of Christianity and Buddhism, although the latter certainly had already established monks and adherents in Central Asia before the Kushans. The Kushans were to establish an imperial tradition in art and culture of Central Asia by uniting various cultural strands, just as they united the tribes and settled folk.

## Notes

1. There are several books with extensive bibliographies regarding this period. Cf. D. Sinor, ed., *The Cambridge History of Early Inner Asia,* especially up to p. 176. Also of note is J. Harmatta, ed., *History of Civilizations of Central Asia,* vol. 2 (Paris: UNESCO, 1994), where detailed bibliographies may be found.
2. V. Sarinidi, *L' or de la Bactriane,* op. cit., passim.

# CHAPTER 9

# The Forgotten Kushans

Before archaeological excavations in our times, the Kushan Empire was one of the forgotten states of history. In Western sources, except several Armenian histories, the name Kushan does not even appear. Rare notices of Bactrians may be found, but neither in Classical nor in later Islamic sources does the eastern counterpart of the Parthians and Sasanians play a role in history. Yet it was with the Kushans that much of Roman trade with India flourished, especially after the discovery of the monsoon winds across the Indian Ocean about the beginning of our era. For more than a century the "great" Kushan kings paralleled the Later Han Empire of China, the Parthians, and the Roman Empire, and in some writings, under the sobriquet of Bactrians, they represented one of the four great monarchies of the age. Perhaps because they were intimately bound with India, where historical traditions were so weak, the Kushans were forgotten. Yet the Kushan rulers established a new chain of legitimacy of rule, following the model of Cyrus and the Achaemenids, and then Alexander and the Greeks. Even late Medieval rulers of Kashmir claimed descent from the Kushan kings, as a measure of their right to rule. After the Kushans themselves had vanished, other rulers called themselves Kushans on their coins.

Aside from the coins and archaeological remains, including inscriptions, we have very little to reconstruct a history of the Kushans and their successors. Several international congresses on the Kushans have failed to bring agreement on the dates of the Kushan rulers, and we only have a relative chronology, based on a sequence of dates in inscriptions, not an absolute chronology.[1] Nonetheless, we may try to establish a plausible scenario for the dates of the rulers, and the extent of Kushan domains in Central Asia, as well as a brief indication of their rule in India.

The *Han Shu,* official history of the Han dynasty of China, in its earlier and later versions, tells us about the formation of the Kushan state.[2] One problem with this and all Chinese sources is that they were written after the events described and have been re-worked, so that sometimes it is impossible to determine what period of time is being discussed. Since we have no other sources, however, at least we may accept the general outlines of the narratives, and interpolate what we find with the evidence of coins and brief notices in Classical sources.

After the fall of king Heliocles' Bactrian kingdom, called Ta-hsia in Chinese sources, the Yüeh-chih established five principalities in their domains, one of which was called Kushan (Kuei-shuang). We may infer from the early Han history (ch. 96) that presumably these principalities were ruled by five tribes or chiefs (*yabghu* = *hsi-hou*), but the majority of the population was composed of settled Bactrians, and Greeks or others, who had migrated from the west. According to the later Han chronicle (ch. 118), more than a century passed after the end of the central Bactrian Greek kingdom, ca. 130 B.C.E. Then the prince of the Kushan principality took over the other four and established the Kushan Empire, after which he conquered Kabul (Kao-fu) from the Parthians, as well as other lands to the south of the Hindukush. The date of the formation of the Kushan state is uncertain, but it should be some years after the beginning of our era.

The ruler who began the process is called Ch'iu-chiu-ch'üeh and is probably to be identified with the Kujula Kadphises of coins. On some of his coins we find that he was associated, in some manner of rule, with a Greek king called Hermaeus, usually called the last Greek king of the Hindukush region. Kujula is said to have ruled eighty years, which is not impossible, since from the number and variety of his coins he must have had a long reign, although the number eighty seems exaggerated. He was followed by Yen-kao-chen, who has been identified as Vima Kadphises, probably his grandson. Then, because of internal troubles, Chinese information about events in the Kushan Empire ceases, although there are stray notes about Kushan intervention in the affairs of eastern Turkestan at the time of the Chinese general Pan Ch'ao about 90 C.E., when the Chinese defeated a Kushan army. There is no evidence, however, for Kushan rule in eastern Turkestan, although some localities may have claimed Kushan protection. What is the testimony of the coins about the rulers?

Numismatists have reconstructed the sequence of rulers, based on their coinage, as follows: one of the princes of the Yüeh-chih confederation, which existed before, or at the time of, Kujula Kadphises, struck coins, and these have been identified as those of a certain Heraus, although the legend is unclear. From find sites of his coins, he ruled in Bactria, or at least the northern part. Then there are a large number of coins of a ruler who calls himself *soter megas,* "great savior," and these were until recently assigned either to the late rule of Kujula, or to early issues of Vima Kadphises, or possibly even another unknown ruler between the two. The last suggestion seemed plausible, otherwise Kujula and Vima would have ruled more than a century between them.

Thanks to a newly discovered inscription in the Bactrian language from Northern Afghanistan, reported by Nicholas Sims-Williams at a meeting of the Societas Iranologica Europaea in Cambridge, England in September 1995, this problem is now solved. The inscription, regarding a sanctuary to be built by order of Kanishka, tells us that Kujula was his great-grandfather, Vima "Taktu" his grandfather and Vima Kadphises his father. Thus the previously unknown ruler Vima "Taktu" was surely the one who called himself *soter megas* on his coins. The inscription also gives a list of divinities to be honored, and the first is Nana, possibly the equivalent of Middle Persian Anahita. This inscription will provide other new information on Kanishka and the early Kushan rulers.

Under Vima Kadphises changes occurred, for he was the first Kushan ruler to have struck coins in gold, with the same weight as the Roman *aureus.* His rule would then date from the end of the first century of our era. Given the nature of the times, we may suggest that the system of vassal rulers and

135

satraps of Parthians and Saka rulers continued under the Kushans, although it is possible that there was a practice of double kingship, or senior and junior rulers, as in the Roman Empire after Diocletian. On the coins of Vima Kadphises the predominance of a figure of Siva on the reverses implies that he was a devotee of this Indian deity. With his successor Kanishka, however, further changes occurred.

The first change we notice is the beginning of a new era of time reckoning, starting with the year one of Kanishka, as we learn from inscriptions. When this began is hotly disputed, with dates ranging from 78 C.E., the beginning of a "so-called Saka era" in Indian inscriptions, to the third century of our era. Inasmuch as it is difficult to say when his rule began, the most likely guess is that Kanishka was ruling about 120 C.E. and he continued for at least 23 years, the date of the last inscription in his name.

Another innovation under Kanishka was the change in legends on his coins, from Greek to the local Iranian tongue which we call Bactrian, although some scholars claim that this was begun under Vima Kadphises. This change was not found on Vima's coins, however, which, in my opinion, is crucial to this question. Third, the proliferation of deities represented on Kanishka's coinage—Greek, Iranian and Indian—indicates a religious tolerance, although Buddhist tradition claims Kanishka as a follower of the Buddha. Certainly under the Kushans Buddhism flourished, but seemingly more under later rulers, such as Kanishka II. If we rely on dates in the inscriptions, the successor of Kanishka I may have been Vasishka, who only ruled four years and was succeeded by Huvishka, who ruled from 28 to the year 60 of the era of Kanishka. Some numismatists, however, place Vasishka after Vasudeva, the last of the so-called "great" Kushans. Under Huvishka the Kushan Empire was probably at its apogee. Finds of coins and archaeological remains suggest that the Kushan Empire in Central Asia under this ruler extended up the Oxus River on both sides, but not including the mouth at Choresmia. In Sogdiana local rulers held sway, possibly as vassals of the Kushans, who held Bactria south of the Hissar Mountains as their homeland.

Like so many rulers in Central Asia, the Kushans too coveted the rich plains of India, and the conquests of Vima Kadphises and his successors gave the Kushans control of central as well as northwest India, and part of Kashmir. In Mathura many statues and other remains of the Kushans have been found, and this part of India remained in Kushan hands after the end of the line of "great" Kushan kings which, again according to dates on inscriptions, ended about 99 years after Kanishka's advent, with the last ruler called Vasudeva.

At the time of the Kushan rulers, the Parthians held not only their homeland around Nisa, but also the oasis of Merv and probably Herat and Sistan under vassal chiefs. The situation in southern Afghanistan and Sind is unclear, for under the early Kushans a dynasty of Indo-Parthian rulers with names such as Gondophares, Abdagases and Vonones held sway for many years during the first century. By the time of Kanishka, however, Kushan hegemony seems to have prevailed in that region. On the other hand, on the basis of coin finds, one might conclude that Parthian chieftains continued to exercise authority in parts of what is today southern Afghanistan down to the third century of our era. Both Parthian rule and Kushan control came to an end in the various regions of present Afghanistan with the coming of the Sasanians in the third century. So the Kushans flourished primarily in the second century.

The second century of our era was unfortunately a dark period in the entire east, yet a period when many changes were imminent. In the Near East, Christianity and Judaism were codifying their scriptures and beginning to establish orthodoxy. World or universal religions were being formed, including Zoroastrianism. The universal written languages of Aramaic and Greek were giving way to local writings in the east—Parthian, Middle Persian, Sogdian, Choresmian—all written with alphabets based on Aramaic, and Bactrian written in a modified Greek alphabet. At the same time Latin was challenging the exclusivity of Greek in the Near East. Allegiances and identities were changing, for religion was becoming the hallmark of identification of an individual,

*Figure 9.* Clay figurine of a goddess from Afrasiyab
(old Samarkand), late Kushan period (from V.A. Meshkeris,
Sogdiiskaya Terrakota, Dushanbe, 1989, 117)

rather than being simply the subject of a certain ruler. Mystery cults and philosophies abounded, but in Central Asia it seems the old order of local cults and beliefs was still in vogue, at first challenged by Buddhism, and only later by other universal religions, including that bane of other religions, Manichaeism.

Just as the line of Greek kings eventually disappeared in India, so did the line of Kushan rulers. After the "great" Kushan kings of the Kanishka century, we find only minor potentates in the subcontinent, but what happened in Bactria, the homeland? According to inscriptions, there may have been a Kanishka II ruling a short time during the Kanishka century, but his dates are uncertain, as is his relation to the dynasty. From the coinage, numismatists have postulated a later Vasudeva and possibly even a Vasudeva III. We are not concerned with the fortunes of later Kushan princelings in India, however, and should return to Central Asia.

From archaeological excavations it is clear that under the "great" Kushans irrigation and agriculture greatly increased in Central Asia, even more than under their predecessors. Finds of Chinese lacquer, Indian carved ivories, Hellenistic (probably from Egypt) glass, and plaster plaques with Greek busts on them, at Begram south of the Hindukush Mountains, reveal the far-flung trading contacts and the prosperity of the Kushan Empire. Other sites, such as Dalverzin and Khalchayan in northern Bactria, had wall paintings and sculptures which rival Begram in richness of culture.

According to archaeologists, in this period irrigation systems all over Central Asia attained their highest level of development, and crops, including vineyards with wine making, proliferated. Details of such handicrafts as the manufacture of weapons (swords, armor, and bows and arrows), textiles, bronze and other metal objects, and ceramics, would require many more pages, while architectural features, including large palaces, fortifications and temples, also reveal the high level of material culture reached under the Kushans. Central Asia prospered, and this state of affairs

*Figure 10*. Kanishka statue,
Mathura Museum

continued, even under the invasions of the post-Kushan age.

One of the factors which created this prosperity was the monetary policy of the Kushans, and the contrast with the period before the reform of Vima Kadphises is striking. In the early period before Kujula, poor copies of the coins of Eucratides and Heliocles were struck, frequently in debased silver. The portraits of the Greek rulers degenerated and were replaced by the busts of local rulers, while the Greek legends became more and more corrupt.

Vima and his successors abandoned the traditional portrait of the ruler on the obverse of coins, and instead depicted a sitting or standing figure, presumably a ruler, wearing a heavy coat and boots, before a small altar. This apparel was the hallmark of the Central Asian Kushan kings. On the reverse of each coin one of a variety of deities became the norm. Gold and copper coins were struck in place of the usual silver coins, and the great number of copper coins reveals an active local monetary economy. The fact that the Parthians, western neighbors of the Kushans, only had silver coins suggests that the Kushans were more attuned to trading and economic development in general. Choresmia at this time at first followed the Parthians, with silver coins imitating the coins of Eucratides, but later they minted their own coins, then followed the Kushans with copper coinage, and the oasis of Merv followed the same pattern.

In Sogdiana coins were struck on the model of those of Euthydemus, but later changing to local issues, while Chach also issued local coins. The change to a gold standard by the Kushans, although primarily directed at trade with India and the Roman Empire, had an effect throughout Central Asia to China where Kushan gold coins were accepted in commercial transactions, probably only by weight. It is also likely that the change to gold was intended to isolate the Parthians, who retained silver. In any case, the prosperity of the Kushans soon extended to its northern neighbors. It should be noted that barbarous imitations of coins could be either official issues or pirated copies, and frequently it is difficult to decide which.

Since there is very little in written sources about social classes and land ownership, we must interpolate from later periods when more information is available. Throughout Central Asia agricultural land was owned by the ruler or the government, by the aristocracy, by temples, or by communes or villages, and rarely by ordinary individuals. Pastoral lands were usually under the control of tribes, although the government might lay claim even to lands only fit for flocks.

Since the Kushan state held sway over many towns, and urbanization was relatively advanced, in comparison with the period of the nomadic migrations, we may suppose the existence of a bureaucracy with an army, and organized taxation. From titles in inscriptions, and from information especially from Indian and Chinese sources, we may attempt an incomplete reconstruction of Kushan administration.

If we begin with the emperor, the title of king of kings appears in the Greek, Bactrian and Indian languages on coins or inscriptions. This inflated title implies a system of

141

*Figure 11.* Kushan stone construction,
Guldara monastery near Kabul

local rulers, who had a good measure of power and authority left to them, as one would expect in such a huge and diverse empire. Closer to Bactria, and also on the plains of India, local authority would be in the hands of satraps or officers appointed by the Kushan emperor, but in more outlying and mountainous areas vassal rulers probably accepted some kind of Kushan hegemony.

The title *devaputra*, literally "son of god," in Prakrit legends on some coins of the "great" Kushans, parallels the Chinese title *t'ien-tzu*, "son of heaven," of their emperors and fits the spirit of late Hellenism, but it does not mean that the Kushan rulers were considered to be divine. It is quite possible, however, that the Kushan emperors copied their Roman counterparts in the West and instituted a cult of the ruler, as shrines with statues of the rulers at Surkh Kotal and

Mathura in India would imply. Perhaps the cult was dedicated only to dead rulers, like the widespread cult of rituals on behalf of one's ancestors. The change in the west from Hellenistic concepts of religion to universal religions had not reached the Kushans, but with syncretism in full force, the way was prepared for the universal religions to slowly absorb the plethora of local religious traditions.

Buddhism, as the first of the universal religions to spread in Central Asia, probably on the whole did not conflict with local cults, but may have been regarded as a philosophy or way of life parallel to, or in conjunction with, the cults. As mentioned earlier in this chapter, from his coins one may say that Vima showed special partiality for the Indian deity Siva, while Vasudeva, from his name, seems to have had an inclination towards Vishnu. Kanishka, or possibly Kanishka II, was regarded in Buddhist texts as a fervent follower of Buddha, and one may conclude that Buddhism not only was tolerated, but at times even supported, so that it spread, especially in eastern Turkestan. The spread of Buddhism in Central Asia will be treated later.

It is unknown but probable that the emperor had some kind of a council to advise him. Directly responsible to the emperor were generals of the army (*kara-lrango* of the Bactrian inscription of Surkh Kotal) and military officers such as the *kanarang* (probably meaning "warden of the marches"). Civil officials undoubtedly existed, most of whom were continuations from earlier periods, but it seems likely that the Kushans retained local administrations wherever they ruled. It is reasonable to suppose that the situation in India would not have been the same as in Bactria, where we may speculate that nomadic traditions played a greater role in institutions of control than in India. Beyond these few snippets, unfortunately, we have no information about the central administrative structure of the empire.

There also is not enough evidence to reconstruct a picture of the local administration in various parts of the empire, but inasmuch as we find a feudal society in the Parthian realm and in the eastern provinces of the Roman Empire, we may infer that such was also the case with the Kushans. This

*Figure 12.* Kushan costume,
Mathura Museum

would further imply a hierarchy of authority, from village leaders up to town and provincial officials, under the satrap or local ruler. It is also unknown how the judicial authority was separated from military or administrative functions, but we may assume the existence of a large number of officials whose exact duties are unknown. For example, the title *dandanayaka* in Indian sources of the Kushan period has been explained as a chief of police, general of the army, judge, or otherwise. In Central Asia, on the other hand, we have no writings and nothing to determine the nature of local government, and a duplicate of local conditions in India cannot be presumed.

In society, obviously the caste system of India did not obtain in Central Asia, where the freer social organization of nomadic society may even have had some influence on settled societies. There we must ask whether nomads maintained a separate existence outside of, but in relation to, the settled areas, as in later times. Pastoralists undoubtedly existed, but did tribal groups exercise any power in the governance of the

144

empire? It seems that under the "great" Kushans they did not, and only long after the fall of the Kushan Empire to the Sasanians, at the time of new nomadic invasions in the fourth century of our era, did the pendulum swing back to nomadic power in rule.

Although written sources on the Kushans are exceedingly meager, the significant lasting monument which we have from them is art. As a result of many excavations of Kushan sites, or Kushan strata in other sites, the picture of art and architecture under their rule is becoming clearer than heretofore. In the beginning of the Kushan Empire we find a combination of Hellenistic, nomadic, local and Indian styles in the art remains. Later under the "great" Kushans, however, two strands dominate the field: imperial art and Buddhist art. The former is well revealed by distinctive statues of the Kushan emperors in heavy coats and boots, especially, as noted, at Surkh Kotal and Mathura. In architecture as well as art, the desire to show imperial power, as under the Achaemenids, is a leitmotif of the Kushan rulers. Local traditions in art, of course, continued to exist, although they were influenced not only by imperial art styles but also by other local schools in the large empire.

As a first question, we may ask how architecture and city planning differed under the Kushans from the Greek and Indian traditions of their predecessors. In Central Asia the Greek city plan was modified by the need for defense against nomadic invaders, typically with a strong citadel and very thick walls around it, as well as around the city. Then we find that larger mud bricks were used than before, and in the mountains where stones were plentiful, a distinctive form of "diaper" construction of walls is found. (This building style had a mixture of large and small stones tightly pressed together without mortar.) The typical features of a Greek city—gymnasium, theater, central square, etc.—seem to have vanished. Temples evolved from their Greek prototype into a central cult room surrounded by corridors, although variations existed. With the spread of Buddhism, typically Buddhist structures appear: *stupas, viharas*, and shrines with Buddha or Bodhisattva figures in them. So the architec-

*Figure 13.* Kushan donors to a Buddhist shrine (from I.T. Kruglikova,
Drevnyaya Baktriya, vol. 2, Moscow, 1979, 123)

ture of Central Asia shows many variations, as well as adherence to past styles and techniques.

The shift in the west from a naturalistic Greek portrayal of human beings to formal, hieratic Parthian poses reached the Kushan domains later than in the west. But Central Asia had another important influence: India, with its sinuous depiction of the female body in statues and carvings. The intertwining of many strands made the art of Central Asia at this time more complex than in Iran proper. The second important strand in Kushan art was Buddhist art.

The art style called Gandharan, after its supposed place of origin, is a Buddhist art which developed parallel to Kushan dynastic art. Scholars suggest that it began with the change from symbolic features, such as the wheel, to a portrayal of the Buddha figure in human form, influenced by Greek canons of art. Another Buddhist style seems to have started in the region of Mathura, but that is part of Indian art history. The flowering of Gandharan art, however, took

146

place under the Kushans, when it spread through Afghanistan into western Turkestan and then to eastern Turkestan with the spread of Buddhism. On the way it was transformed into local variations, best revealed in the spectacular wall paintings of Kyzyl, Bezeklik and elsewhere. The interactions of the many strands and phases of art in Central Asia for years have fascinated art historians, and the picture we have today is clearer, but vastly more complex, than envisioned over fifty years ago when it was thought that Buddhism had not penetrated west of a line drawn from Balkh through Bamiyan. With the general outline now apparent, only details need to be filled to create a fuller picture of local variations of the overall scheme.

## Decline and Fall of the Kushans

It is thought that after Vasudeva I the empire of the "great" Kushans ended when the Sasanians conquered their Bactrian homeland and western parts of the Kushan empire. The dating of inscriptions in the era of Kanishka ends, and we can only speculate about the consequences of Sasanian victories. The Arabic history of Tabari, followed by other late sources, tells us that the first Sasanian king Ardashir, after his defeat of the Parthians and assertion of his authority in the west, turned to Sistan, Gurgan, Parthia (called Abarshahr), Merv, Balkh and Khwarazm, to the farthest borders of Khurasan, after which he returned to Gor (present Firuzabad) in Fars. To him came the kings of the Kushans, of Turan and of Makran to offer their submission. Even though there may be some exaggeration, the basic information that Ardashir campaigned in the east in the 230s need not be doubted.

The inscription of his son and successor Shapur I, over thirty years later on the Ka'ba of Zoroaster at Naqsh-e Rustam in Fars province, tells us that the empire which he ruled included Turan, Makuran, Paradene, Hindustan, and the Kushanshahr (Kushan state) up to Peshawar, and (in the north) to Kesh, Sogdiana and to the mountains of Chach (Tashkent). We assume that the last three above mentioned lands were not tributary or subject to Shapur, but the former places were. Their identification is not without problems, but we may locate them as follows: Turan of medieval Arabic geographies is probably the area of present day Kalat in Baluchistan. Makuran is undoubtedly the Makran coast to the south of Turan, while Paradene may be the region of present Quetta. Hindustan is surely part of Sind province, but how much is unknown.

The boundaries of the Kushan empire, or that part claimed by Shapur, extended up to but not including the lowlands of Peshawar in the east, and up to the Hissar range, beyond which were located Kesh, Sogdiana and the low mountains of the Tashkent region to the north. A tentative clarification of this information implies the division of the Kushan Empire already before Shapur (possibly in the time of his father) into at least two parts: the Indian realm, and Bactria with the mountain areas of Central Asia. Further, the uncertainty in the wording implies that north of the Hissar mountains of Bactria, the lands of the Kashka Darya, of Sogdiana, and of settlements in the mountains south of the plain of Tashkent, may have been in some sort of loose relationship with the Kushan state to the south, which the author of the inscription left vague. There is no mention in the inscription of a Sasanian governor of the Kushan domains, so we may conclude that the series of Kushano-Sasanian rulers who struck coins had not begun when the inscription was made, probably in the late 260s.

How and when Sasanian governors replaced the Kushan rulers of Bactria is uncertain, but a good guess would place the beginning of integration of at least the northern part of the Kushan realm into the Sasanian Empire about 270 at the end of the reign of Shapur. Until towards the end of the next century the Sasanians ruled the homeland of the Kushans, either from Balkh or from Merv, since their coins were struck in both places. But the governors kept the titles "King of the Kushans," "Great King," or even "King of Kings of the Kushans." The last title is found on the coins of Hormizd, probably that brother of the Sasanian king Bahram II who is said to have revolted in the east after the latter's accession in 276.

148

The Sasanian princes who ruled the Kushan realm have been placed in chronological order by numismatists on the basis of style, especially their crowns, on their coins in the following order: Ardashir I Kushanshah, Peroz I, Hormizd I Kushanshahanshah, Hormizd II, Peroz II, Bahram I and Bahram II.[4] Their coins were in gold and copper, except for a small issue in silver by Peroz and Hormizd, and the coins either followed the thick Kushan style (in Balkh?) or the thin Sasanian style (in Merv?). Since coins of the Kushano-Sasanians have been found along the banks of the Oxus River, we may assume that they exercised some kind of hegemony over this region as did the Kushans before them. Different local coinages in Sogdiana and Choresmia, however, point to the independence of small states in the various oases. The Kushano-Sasanians probably ruled for little more than a century, but in that time Sasanian customs and knowledge of the Persian language spread in Bactria, although Bactrian was not displaced. This seems to have been the beginning of the change in Central Asia from local languages to Persian, completed by the later Arab conquests.

How far Sasanian jurisdiction spread south of the Hindukush Mountains is unknown, for no written sources exist. Under the aggressive ruler Shapur II (309–379), who campaigned in the east with varying fortunes, the Sasanians probably obtained the submission of some of the peoples living in the mountains of Afghanistan, but after his death nomadic invaders again wrested control from the Sasanians of much of their eastern possessions.

# Notes

1. Of great value for the study of the Kushans are the annotated bibliographies by G. Fussman in the *Journal Asiatique* in 1978 and especially his "Chronique des études Kouchanes (1978–87)" in *JA* 275, nos. 3–4, 331–400. Publications of the two international conferences are: A.L. Basham, *Papers on the Date of Kaniṣka* (Leiden: E.J. Brill, 1968), and B.G. Gafurov, ed., *Central Asia in the Kushan Period*, 2 vols. (Moscow, 1974–75), in Russian and English. For a bibliography see B.N. Puri, *Kuṣāna Bibliography* (Calcutta: Naya Prokash, 1977), and M. Stwodah,

*Kushans, Annotated Bibliography*, 2 vols. (Kabul, 1978), in English and Persian. For matters of Kushan rule in India consult B.N. Puri, *India under the Kushānas* (Bombay: Bharatiya Vidya Bhavan, 1965), and the many books of Bratindra Nath Mukherjee, professor at the University of Calcutta.

2. For a translation of all the Chinese texts dealing with the Kushans see E. Zürcher, "The Yüeh-chih and Kaniṣka in the Chinese Sources," in Basham, op. cit., 346–393.

3. Cf. A. Mukhamedjanov, "Economy and Social system in Central Asia in the Kushan Age," in J. Harmatta, ed., *History of Civilizations of Central Asia*, vol. 2, 270.

4. Cf. J. Cribb, "Numismatic evidence for Kushano-Sasanian chronology," *Studia Iranica* 19 (1990), 151–93. The absolute dates of rule for the Kushan governors in the east are much disputed, but a good guess would place them from about 270 to 360.

# CHAPTER 10

# The Silk Route

In 1877 the German geographer von Richthofen coined the term "Silk Route" to describe the trade route from China to the west in antiquity, for silk was the most valuable textile and the most desired article of trade from China to the west. It was so important that the land of Seres (from Greek *ser*, "silk worm") became a designation in the world of Greece and Rome for the land of silk's origin, which was China, although Greek and Roman knowledge of the Far East was decidedly unclear.

With the breakup of the Soviet Union and the opening of China, the expression "Silk Route" became such a fad that UNESCO organized a multi-faceted program of conferences, exhibitions and expeditions around the theme of the "Silk Route." Many books and articles were published on this subject which included not only the routes across the continent of Asia but also the sea routes between east and west.[1] Such has been the influence of this concept in the modern economic and commercial world that the history of ancient and medieval Central Asia is dominated by the vision of international trade over the vast distances between China and western Europe. We should review the various facets of Central Asian history connected with the "Silk Route."

The discovery of the silkworm and consequent weaving of textiles from the silk fibres of its cocoons is attested from the third millennium B.C.E. by Chinese records. The entire process of sericulture was kept a secret by the Chinese for many centuries and outsiders did not learn about the process by which the worms were fed mulberry leaves and the manner in which silk cloth was created until the early centuries of our era. In both Japan and lands of the west silk production began late, although India seems to have been an exception, for silk production is reported in early Sanskrit literature.

The stories about the introduction of the silk worm to India and to the Byzantine Empire are strikingly parallel. In both cases the worms were smuggled: into India, concealed in the headdress of a Chinese princess, while monks brought the worms to Byzantium hidden in canes. But the trade in Chinese silks was much earlier than the production of silk outside China.

Just as oil is the liquid gold of the present, so silk was the most important article not only of trade but also of payment in China. Nomads were persuaded to stop their raids by presents of rolls or bolts of silk from the Chinese court. Likewise special services by individuals to the Chinese state were rewarded with gifts of silk. The production of silk was closely controlled by Chinese authorities, and even after the spread of sericulture elsewhere, Chinese silk remained highly prized because of its superior quality and intricate designs.

Aristotle mentions silk produced by a worm but obviously knew no details about the production of the light but strong and pleasant textile.[2] In Rome silk clothing was highly prized and very expensive, and it was not until the increased demand by the wealthy inhabitants of the Roman Empire that we can speak of the flowering of the "Silk Route." The early Roman Empire coincided with the rise of the Kushans, and this period may be characterized as the real beginning of the "Silk Route" from China to the Roman Empire.

International trade expanded enormously during the Kushan period, and in Central Asia the Sogdians were the merchants who took advantage of the demand for silk in the west, and for horses, jade and spices in China, as well as for gold in India. Various pharmaceuticals were also important articles of trade through Central Asia. North-south trade routes also began to function in this period, with furs and honey from Russia and amber from the Baltic sought by peoples in the south in exchange for handicrafts such as silver plates and ewers. This trade, however, greatly developed only several centuries after the Kushans. It should be noted that slaves were always an important commodity of purchase and sale in all societies of the time.

*Figure 14.* Kushan costume on coin, Foroughi collection

Not only did domestic slaves exchange hands in the market places of the ancient and medieval world, but various people headed towards the rich Chinese lands, especially at the
time of the T'ang dynasty. The Chinese, especially at court,
sought dancers, acrobats, and especially musicians from the
west, for their entertainment. Kucha early became famous as
a source of desirable musicians, and Central Asian instru-
ments, such as two and three stringed lutes, were prized in
Chinese society. Also, exotic animals such as the ostrich were
taken long distances to the Chinese court. In short, the "Silk
Route" was an international trading system with many different wares going in various directions; it was not just one
road between China and the west. The various political entities of the time, from the later Han to the end of the T'ang
dynasties in China (first century B.C.E. to the tenth century
C.E.) profited from the expanded trade but were jealous of the

155

profits to be secured.

Competition between Roman, Parthian, and Central Asian merchants was keen and influenced political relations between the states. The Parthians, followed by the Sasanians, tried to monopolize the silk trade to the west by controlling the overland routes, and the peoples of Central Asia sought to circumvent obstacles, such as high tariffs for passage, through the Parthian and then Sasanian territories. Although both Indian and Sogdian trading colonies existed in eastern Central Asia, the former along the southern arm of the "Silk Route" through Yarkand and Khotan eastwards, while the Sogdians favored the northern road through Kucha and Turfan, as time went on the Sogdians became more active than their Indian counterparts, most of whom were absorbed into the local population. The Sogdians, however, seem to have maintained their identity over a long period of time until the spread of Islam.

Especially interesting in this regard are the Sogdian "Ancient Letters," dating from shortly after 311 C.E., found in a Chinese watchtower at the western edge of the limes built by the Chinese as an extension of the "Great Wall" against nomads.[3] They reveal a well-developed trade route with intermediate stations between China and the Sogdian principalities and Bactria, which had a great development in the Kushan period. This is not to imply that there was only one physical route, but that both geography and political stability in Central Asia determined the selection of roads by merchants. In general it seems that merchants coming from Bactria preferred to follow the Amu Darya northwards in the winter, and even in the summer if the heat did not deter them. In the spring and autumn, however, they went over the Hissar Mountains and other ranges because of the milder weather and availability of supplies for both themselves and their beasts of burden, primarily the "Bactrian" two-humped camel. The "Arabian" one-humped dromedary later spread eastward gradually replacing their relatives in western Central Asia. Horses, especially from Ferghana, called "blood-sweating" in Chinese sources, were especially prized by the Chinese.

If in the steppes a state existed which maintained control over the routes through its domains, and provided aid for caravans, then merchants might prefer to travel in the north, in place of the difficult mountain passes over the Karakorum or the Himalayas to India, or the Wakhan road to Bactria. The Turkic empire of the seventh century is an example of such a control of the steppe route by one power, but none had the far-flung control and stability of the Mongol Empire of the thirteenth century. Most of the time the oasis states of the Tarim basin provided the best access to China by way of the Gansu corridor and we should turn to them.

# Notes

1. There are many publications that deal with the Silk Route, especially photograph albums and exhibition catalogues. See, e.g., for the latter, *Along the Ancient Silk Routes, Central Asian Art from the West Berlin State Museums*, (New York: Metropolitan Museum, 1982). Among the former see C. Thubron, *The Silk Road* (New York, 1989). A general and detailed account is by H. Klimkeit, *Die Seidenstrasse* (Cologne: DuMont, 1988). In Tehran there is even a journal called *Silk Road*, published in English.
2. Aristotle, *Historia Animalium,* V.19 (17) and 11(6). His uncertain account about silk remained the basis of knowledge in the west about sericulture throughout the period of the Roman Empire.
3. For the Sogdian "Ancient Letters" see F. Grenet and N. Sims-Williams, "The Historical Context of the Sogdian Ancient Letters," *Transition Periods in Iranian History*, Studia Iranica, Cahier 5 (Paris, 1987), 101–122.

# CHAPTER 11

# The Buddhist East

Eastern Turkestan has been neglected because the small oasis states of the Tarim basin did not play a role on the world stage of history comparable to the Sogdians, Bactrians and Khwarazmians, whose trading activities brought them in contact with three large areas of natural or handicraft products: China, India, and northern Europe. All of the Central Asian peoples, of course, maintained trade connections with the Near East.[1] Sogdian merchants, with the establishment of trading colonies, expanded their activity in the east under the Kushans. Bactrian trade contacts with India began even earlier, while Khwarazmian trading relations with the northwest came later. Merchants from the states of the Tarim basin were not comparable to the Sogdians, either in distance or quantity of trade. For the oases of Kucha, Khotan and others, it was Chinese expansion under the Han dynasty, and then the spread of Buddhism, which brought them to the attention of outside powers.

Buddhist missionaries entered western Central Asia during the Maurya dynasty under its most famous ruler Asoka, and it took root in Bactria. Sogdiana, however, never became a Buddhist center, unlike its southern neighbor. The oases of the Tarim basin however, provided the most fertile ground for Buddhism. Already in the first century Buddhist missionaries had reached Tun-huang and had entered China proper. In addition to Tun-huang, both Kucha and Khotan became great centers of Buddhist learning, where translations of Prakrit or Sanskrit texts were made into local languages, but that was a later development which needs more investigation.

The Vedas of India, which are recited by priests, cannot be translated since the sounds give the message its power, and can only be explained for the adherent of the religion. The same is true for the Qur'an of the Muslims, but the Buddhist religious texts are only the responses of the historical Buddha to problems of this world; they do not contain divine revelations. Consequently the ideas rather than the exact words of the Buddha should be transmitted to posterity, and in the ancient Indian context that meant orally. By the time of Asoka, however, Buddhist teachings were being recorded in various Prakrits, while Sanskrit, the literary language of poets and philosophers, only achieved its dominance in the Gupta period (ca. 327–467 C.E.). What did this mean for Buddhist missionaries to Central Asia?

The missionaries, at first Indians, the majority of whom probably were also merchants, needed some back-up texts when explaining Buddhist doctrines to the peoples of Central Asia, and these were in Prakrit dialects of India, especially in that Prakrit dubbed Gandhari Prakrit, written in the Kharoshthi alphabet, after the presumed place of origin. In fact the earliest Buddhist textual fragments found in Central Asia were written in a Prakrit tongue, and only later in Sanskrit. According to Chinese tradition the first Buddhist missionary to China was a Parthian prince, but no trace of Buddhist literature in the Parthian language has been detected. The same is true of Bactrian, the administrative language of the northern part of the Kushan Empire. Yet according to Buddhist tradition, the Buddha is said to have recommended that his message be translated into vernacular languages. Evidently the Buddhist missionaries followed this precept only as far as the spoken word was concerned, an Indian predilection which was carried to Central Asia. But the attitude of the people of Central Asia, or at least of the local priests, was probably similar to that of their Iranian neighbors in the west: reverence for a sacred book. Furthermore, the sounds of a "sacred" language evidently were important for the people of the eastern oases as in India. This resulted in a cult of the book in later Buddhism, perhaps a tradition which began in Central Asia and spread to India.

This attitude is well expressed by the author of the Buddhist poem written in the old Khotanese language at the request of an official called Zambasta.[2] He says (ch. 23, 4–5): "The Khotanese do not value the Law (Buddhist teachings) at all in Khotanese. They understand it badly in Indian. In Khotanese it does not seem to them to be the Law. For the Chinese the Law is in Chinese." The last sentence shows the difference between the Chinese and the Indian approaches to Buddhist writings; the Chinese at once translated the writings from original Indian texts into Chinese, whereas the Central Asians originally believed that monks should study the originals and explain them to the laity orally, much as in the case of Latin in the Middle Ages in the West. It seems that when the Chinese again extended their rule into Central Asia under the Sui, but especially the T'ang dynasty, the local people of the oases began to copy the Chinese example and began translating the Buddhist texts into Khotanese, Tumshuqese, Kuchean (Tokharian B) and later into Uighur and other languages. The example of the universal and missionary religions of Christianity, Manichaeism, and later Islam, also could have influenced the Central Asians to translate religious texts into their own languages.

Khotan, according to legends in Tibetan texts, and in Chinese pilgrim accounts, was founded by Indian settlers in the time of Asoka, and certainly Indian influence was strong there from early times, but as early as Asoka is uncertain. On bilingual Sino-Kharoshthi coins of the first and second centuries of our era the native name of Khotan—Hvatana—is found. Khotan became a great center of Hinayana Buddhism, but it was not a center of missionary influence on its neighbors, since the many monasteries in Khotan and surroundings were internally oriented, and the Khotanese language never became a vehicle for the propagation of the faith. Later here, as at Kucha, Mahayana Buddhism became popular. The royal family of Khotan, with the name Visya, lasted many centuries until the Muslim conquest of the eleventh century, evidence of the stability of rule in this station on the "Silk Route." Khotan was especially known for its jade, which was much in demand in China.

The northern oases, with their water from the T'ien Shan range, were more productive than the south. The cold winters but hot summers enabled cotton, melons and other warm land produce to bring prosperity to the region. In addition silver and sal ammoniac, used in the preparation of leather, were early mined in the mountains near Kucha. Access to water was a perennial problem, and in the oasis of Turfan underground canals were built from the mountains to keep the water from evaporating. Also Turfan was an oasis with shifting places of settlement, unlike other oases, where the sites of settlement remained more constant. The lack of trees, however, forced people to build with mud or bricks, and no impressive stone structures were erected there.

The northern trade route to the west passed through Hami (Komul), Turfan, Karashahr, Kucha to Kashgar and over the Terek pass to the Ferghana valley, and all of the oasis states flourished because of trade. Because of competition, or for other reasons, the oasis states were rarely able to unite or even cooperate, and conflicts between them were a recurring feature of the history of this area. The nomads of the north and China to the east took advantage of the oasis disputes to further their own policies.

At the time of the Han dynasty, China not only conquered eastern Turkestan and installed garrisons there, but also it was the beginning of Chinese migration into the area, first in the Gansu corridor, then at Tun-huang and farther west. Contacts between this area and China were maintained after the fall of the Han dynasty, but not until the Sui and T'ang did the Chinese again occupy the oases, although minor Chinese dynasties at times exercised some influence on internal affairs in eastern Turkestan. It must have been difficult for the Chinese, both civilians and soldiers, to live in the west, and T'ang poets tell of the loneliness and trials of Chinese garrisons stationed there.

It was during the T'ang dynasty that Chinese influence was at its height in the west, and Chinese arts and crafts were much admired by foreigners who flocked to the T'ang court at Ch'ang-an. In the Chinese annals embassies from the countries of the west were regularly regarded as tribute bringers from barbarian lands, since the Chinese regarded themselves as living in the center of the world with the highest culture of all. This attitude has not changed throughout the ages.

Archaeological discoveries in the Tarim basin have greatly increased our knowledge of the material culture of the
oasis states. The common culture of the oases was more
Chinese influenced and oriented in the eastern oases than in
the west, where Kashgar, for example, was much more akin
to Samarkand than to Tun-huang. Of all the oases, Kashgar
seems to have been the least influenced by Buddhism, for
Buddhist remains are few there. This may be because
Kashgar was the first oasis conquered by the Muslim
Karakhanid Turks at the end of the tenth century, who may
have destroyed most vestiges of Buddhism. But also before
that time, Kashgar had been conquered commercially by
Sogdian merchants, who were not inclined towards
Buddhism. As a matter of fact, the preserved Sogdian
Buddhist texts we have were for the most part translated
from Chinese, since Chinese monks became the authorities
for Buddhist doctrines in Central Asia. There were Nestorian
Christian and Manichaean communities in the oases of the
Tarim basin, the fragmentary texts of whom have been found
written in several languages, but Buddhism remained the
most prominent of the religions, and in the eleventh century
it was the adversary of Islam.

To the north of the T'ien Shan the land was mostly fit for
pastoralism, except the agriculturally rich Ili valley, the old
home of the Wu-sun. The Wu-sun, as noted, were probably
those known in western sources as As and Alans, part of the
Sarmatian confederacy and ancestors of the Ossetes.
Unfortunately no archaeological investigations have been
made in the Ili valley, and we are reduced to conjectures
about the history of that valley. Inasmuch as the Hiung-nu
exercised control over the Ili region for a long time, we may
suppose that Altaic speaking nomads had mixed with the
ancient inhabitants, soon replacing the Indo-European
tongues with Altaic languages. The rich valley, with the
neighboring Altai Mountains, became a center of nomadic
power for various tribes until the rise of the Avars and Turks
in the sixth century, but that is part of the next scenario in
the history of Central Asia.

# Notes

1. On Xinjiang in this period cf. L. Hambis, ed., *L'Asie Centrale* (Paris: Imprimerie nationale, 1977), with bibliography.
2. R.E. Emmerick, *The Book of Zambasta* (Oxford, 1968).

# CHAPTER 12

# Return of the Nomads

The fourth century of our era may be characterized as that of the entry of new nomads on the stage of history, this time Altaic speakers.[1] How did Central Asia look about the year 350?

North China was in a state of disorder with many small states striving for supremacy, many of them ruled by nomadic chiefs who had come from north of the Great Wall. Chinese influence in the west had collapsed, and the oasis states of the Tarim were also subject to attack by nomads from north of the T'ien Shan. Likewise, on the steppes of what is now Kazakhstan, new nomads from the east represented the first wave of Altaic speaking nomads to move from Mongolia westwards. Just as all nomads previously had been called Sakas or Scythians, so the new rulers of the steppes were called Huns. Whether the name Hun is the same as the Chinese Hiung-nu has been hotly debated, but certainly usage of the name Hun succeeded, and parallelled, that of the earlier Hiung-nu. In any case, by 350 Altaic speaking nomads had assumed leadership in the new nomadic confederations which spread to the Sasanian Empire in the south and the Roman Empire in the West.

When we look at the movement of nomads from Mongolia to the west and south, two different types of invasion over the steppes to settled lands may be distinguished. The first is the so-called "billiard-ball" model, where one tribe impinges on its neighbor, whereupon that tribe moves against a more distant tribe, and the last tribe then spills over onto the settled land. One example of that model in the pre-Achaemenid period would be the Scythians pushing the Cimmerians into Anatolia; another, the Yüeh-chih pushing the Sakas ahead of them to the south into Sistan. In both cases we assume that is what happened.

169

The other kind of nomadic movement may be called one of penetration, or passing through other tribes, and is revealed by the invasion of Europe by the Huns, who are supposed to have come from Mongolia, and moved across Eurasia into Hungary at the end of the fourth century. The invasion of the Near East and Europe by the Mongols in the 13th century would be another example of this kind of invasion. Actually in both cases, other tribes or remnants of defeated tribes were joined to the confederacy created by the movement of the conquering group, so they cannot be considered pure examples of penetration.

Among most nomads from the steppes a strict hierarchy of tribes seems to have existed, whereby a "ruling clan," or what might be called a "charismatic clan," was recognized by others as having the right to provide a leader whom other clans would follow. Other tribes, related by language or ties of kinship, would provide support to any charismatic leader of the tribe with the ruling clan, either willingly or by force, after being defeated. The new confederation then would co-opt neighboring tribes, usually by force, and finally settled people would be conquered and integrated into what had become a steppe empire. Usually such a steppe empire or confederation would not outlast the death of the founder, although with a strong brother or son to succeed the founder, the organization could last longer than a lifetime. The practice of a brother succeeding a leader was not rare on the steppes, for seniority in a family or clan was frequently followed, especially if a son were too young or seemed unequal to the task of leadership. Names of tribes also changed, especially when a particularly important leader exercised exceptional power and acquired prestige. The name of the Hephthalites, for example, according to Chinese sources, was given to a tribe after the name of its most prominent leader.

In the middle of the fourth century tribes were on the move again in the steppes from the presumed homeland of the Huns in Mongolia. The Huns could be said to have followed both patterns of movement, by reaching far into Central Europe and by driving other peoples ahead of them. The invasion of Europe by the Hunnic confederation, headed

*Figure 15.* Yavan, stamp on fragment of jar, Sasanian potentate,
4th cent. C.E.

by Attila, driving the Ostrogoths and others ahead of them, is
not our concern here, but we may suppose a parallel movement of tribes into Sogdiana, Bactria and Iran at this time.
One question immediately arises. Were the people who invaded Iran, and are called Chionites in various sources, the same
people who invaded Europe; was there only a small ruling
group of Huns over a federation, or had they no connection
with the Huns, and only took the name to frighten their enemies? The second alternative makes the most sense, although
it is only a guess, and we may regard this nomadic group as
one of the last of Iranian-speaking nomads, mixed with Altaic
speakers who were called Huns. The name Chionite is related to, and may be a variant pronunciation of, Hun.[2] But the
word Chionite has problems, since in the Avesta a cognate
word *hyaona* appears, which must be older than the advent
of the Huns. Also in Ptolemy's geography (book II.5.25) the
Hunoi appear as a people living in south Russia. But these
apparent variants of the name Hun probably only mean the

171

existence of similar sounding names from early times, and should not be identified necessarily with the Huns of the fourth century, who came from the direction of Mongolia.

One may characterize the period from the end of the empire of the "great" Kushans as the decline of cities, and the growth of villages and large estates, with castles in the countryside in Central Asia. It seems that more and more authority and power was shifting to local lords from a central government, and under the Kushano-Sasanian governors this process was not halted, but the position of the nomads in the process is unclear. In any case, the stability of "great" Kushan rule was gone and a confused period of history ensued.

The proliferation of imitations of Kushan coins, mostly debased gold coins, and then from about 260 C.E. silver coins on the Sasanian model, indicates economic uncertainty, if not actual decline. The dates and areas of circulation of various coins are difficult to determine, and we are reduced again to speculation. The fact that coins of the Sasanian Shapur II have been found in hoards as far east as Pakistan may indicate Sasanian rule for a time even over the plains of northwest India.[3] But Sasanian coins were receiving a reputation for purity of silver and absence of debasement, which may have extended the sphere of use of such coins beyond the political frontiers of the Sasanian Empire. For example, the discovery of Sasanian coins in excavations in eastern Turkestan certainly does not indicate Sasanian rule there.

In Central Asia at this time we may distinguish three possible sources of rule: the Sasanian government, either directly or through Kushano-Sasanian governors; local lords; or nomadic chiefs. Probably at the beginning, the nomadic invaders allowed either Sasanian governors or local lords to rule, nominally under the aegis of tribal chiefs. Even before that, the nomads first may have served as mercenaries in Sasanian armies, like Germans in the Roman army, as we infer from the account of Grumbates king of the Chionites, serving under Shapur II in his siege of Amida, according to Ammianus (XIX).

The Roman historian Ammianus Marcellinus (XVI.9.4)

tells us that Shapur II was busy fighting the Chionites and other tribes in the year 356, and only two years later, after much struggle, he made an alliance with them. The Chionites were probably accepted for a time as nomadic allies of the Kushano-Sasanian governors of Bactria, but then they brought an end to Sasanian rule in the east. As mentioned, the name Kushan continues in usage, and coins struck with this designation on them may indicate actual descent from earlier Kushan monarchs, or local lords, or nomadic chiefs simply availing themselves of the prestige of the name.

The Sasanians, however, did not give up claim to Bactria without a struggle, and, from coins, it is possible that Bahram IV (388–399) was king of the Kushans before he became Sasanian king. More likely, however, the Chionites were the real rulers in the east, and they copied the coinage of the Sasanian king. One of the Chionite chiefs about this time, called Kidara, although his dates are quite uncertain, struck coins calling himself king of the Kushans, which coins are found in many sites, especially northwest India. Since the coins are varied and numerous, it has been suggested that there was a dynasty of Kidarite rulers, which is plausible. More confusing, however, are the tribal names which are found in various sources about the Chionites in this period. "White Huns" and "Red Huns," Alkhon, Warz, and other designations have brought forth studies of the etymologies and significance of these names, without any agreement.[4] Without literary sources it is difficult to bring order into the great number of coins which were struck in Central Asia before Islam.

It seems clear, however, that the next century, the fifth, was one of increased movement of a number of Hun tribes, from the northern steppes or from eastern Turkestan, into Bactria and beyond to the Indian lowlands. Undoubtedly Iranian speaking tribes were incorporated into the movement, so that by the next century Altaic speakers have replaced Iranian tribes on the steppes. Henceforth the history of Mongolia, the Altai Mountains, the Ili valley, and the steppes, is that of Turks and Mongols. But everywhere, including the southern part of Central Asia, we find this a dark period of lack of information.[5]

In Sogdiana we have only local coins, which are difficult to date, to aid in a reconstruction of history. In the region of Samarkand we find one series of coins, beginning with an unclear bust and a debased Greek inscription, with an archer on the reverse, and these coins, with no identification of the ruler, continue for several centuries. In the oasis of Bukhara another type of coin was struck, bearing at first the name Hyrkodes in Greek, but rapidly becoming illegible and then anepigraphic. The debased silver coinage seems to have been constantly reduced in weight (and value?) until seemingly a reform occurred, and a new standard, based on Sasanian coins, was introduced in Sogdiana, copying the coins of the Sasanian ruler Bahram IV, and for Bukhara, Bahram V. This is an indication of the prestige as well as the power of the Sasanian Empire in Central Asia, but the question of the extent of Sasanian rule in Central Asia is unclear.[6]

Only one Armenian source mentions the defeat of a Sasanian king, either Shapur III or Bahram IV, in fighting the Kushan ruler of Balkh. The local ruler must have been a Chionite, but a number of Armenian books tell us that the "Kushan" kings of this time were of Arsacid (Parthian) origin. It is conceivable that some Parthian princes, in flight from the Sasanians, took wives from families of Chionite or local chiefs, but we cannot corroborate the Armenian information with any other source.

As expected, the new nomads, like their predecessors, were attracted to the rich and warm plains of India, and kingdoms were founded there. We have not only the name Kidara, and the tribal name Chionite, but others such as War or Avar, Alkhon, etc., and it is difficult to identify and place the various personal names or tribal designations in time and space. But in Central Asia, after the middle of the fifth century, a new name appeared as that of invaders from the east who were to settle and remain: the Hephthalites.

A number of Chinese dynastic histories—the *Liang-shu*, *Pei-shu*, *Sui-shu*, early *T'ang-shu*, and later works—say that the Hephthalites were descendants of the great Yüeh-chih, and they were originally called Hua (ancient Chinese reconstruction: *War), before they adopted the name of one of their chiefs. They wandered from eastern Turkestan to the west about 460 C.E. Since the Chinese at that time were dependent on second-hand information about their western borders, we can only guess that the Hephthalites were another wave of Altaic speaking tribes, originally from the Altai-Mongolia area, who moved across Central Asia to eventually invade India. There is no record of their early history, and we can only say that although the name Chionite still persists, generally it is replaced by Hephthalite.

The situation in Mongolia and the Tarim basin had changed from the time of the Hiung-nu successor states. At the end of the fourth century of our era a new name, Jouan-jouan, appeared as the most important power to the north and northwest of China, but it is only recorded in Chinese sources, and seems to be an appellation instead of a real name. In the early part of the next century these people extended their rule to the oasis states of the Tarim basin, and it is possible that the Hephthalites moved west under pressure from the Jouan-jouan.

A plausible reconstruction of history in western Central Asia would have the Hephthalites ending the rule of their predecessors the Kidarites, whose rulers called themselves Kushans, but who themselves probably were a mixture of local people and Chionites or Huns, as we shall now call them. The bulk of the population, of course, remained Iranian-speaking.

The Hephthalites began to replace the Sogdians as rulers about the middle of the fifth century, but the military and political relations between Hephthalites, Kidarites and Sasanians in this period remain unclear. A Byzantine author, Priskos (CLIII.28), mentions the Kidarite Huns under the rule of a certain Koungas, and it seems he was the last, or near the last, Kidarite ruler in Bactria. Then we may postulate that the forces of the Kidarites, either by defeat or in flight from the Hephthalites, left Bactria and joined their southern brethren in India, but hardly before the beginning of the fifth century. Since written sources do not exist, and the coinage is confused, the extent of rule of the Kidarites and others in northwest India can only be guessed. In any case, from the Persian side, only under Bahram V (420–438) do we find reference to a conflict with the Hephthalites, and unless there is an anachronism, which is always possible for this period, we may consider this time as the beginning of Hephthalite rule in Sogdiana and other eastern lands.

There are several indications of extensive, though ephemeral, conquests by Bahram V in Central Asia. First we have the coins of Bukhara, which for a long time were called Bukhar-Khudat, ostensibly copied from the coins of Bahram. Another is a notice in a late Islamic historian Baihaqi, probably taken from a history of Khwarazm by al-Biruni, which tells of a rule over that country by Bahram V, surnamed Gor. From Arabic histories we read that Bahram defeated the Hephthalites near Kushmaihan in the eastern part of the oasis of Merv, after which he advanced to the Oxus and crossed into the oasis of Bukhara. From finds of his coins, he probably also ruled Bactria, or possibly the Kidarites in Bactria became his vassals. Certainly from his time conflicts between the Sasanians and nomads in the east continued, and until the coming of the Arabs in the seventh century we are in the nomadic period of the history of Central Asia.

There are several interesting features reported about Hephthalite society, one being their reputed polyandry, at least among their rulers when they were in Xinjiang, and another the deformation of skulls. The first is reported in Chinese sources, in several cases of two brothers marrying one wife, or having practices similar to the Tibetans. The lengthening of skulls, by binding them in infancy, may be seen on coins and silver vessels, but this was not peculiar to the Hephthalites, since one may observe the same phenomenon among the Kushans, and especially the Alans.[7] It is possible that this form of head deformation was intended to distinguish the invading nomad ruling class from the settled folk they conquered. In Byzantine sources the Hephthalites are described as having light skins and features unlike the Huns who invaded the Roman Empire. This has led to the theory that the Hephthalites were in fact simply mountaineers of Badakhshan, who used the reputation of the Huns to enhance the reputation of their own ferocity against enemies.[8] Undoubtedly local people played an important role in the Hephthalites domains, but the existence of an element of Huns nonetheless is highly probable.

The Hephthalites had some kind of hegemony over the oasis states of eastern Turkestan, according to Chinese sources, but they do not seem to have moved from Sogdiana south to invade Bactria until sometime about the middle of the fifth century. Yazdgird II (439–57), successor of Bahram, had to fight in the east, but whether against Kidarites or Hephthalites or both is unknown. Under his successor Hormizd III (457–59), however, we are dealing only with the Hephthalites, who now dominate the scene in Bactria and Transoxiana, the land between the Oxus and Jaxartes.

It is clear that the Hephthalites were different from the Huns under Attila who invaded Europe, to a great extent because the Huns of Attila gathered other nomads into their confederation, while the Hephthalites relied on the settled people of Sogdiana and Bactria to manage their empire. The Bactrian script and language was continued under the Hephthalites, and trade and commerce flourished as previously. Merchants from their domains travelled far and wide into China, Mongolia and India with trade in spices and silk ever increasing.

Yet when the Hephthalites, called Hunas in Indian sources, invaded the subcontinent they spread destruction and plundered Buddhist monasteries, as well as dwellings of the settled people. One horde of Hunas was defeated by the Gupta ruler Skandagupta in 454, but the invasion, though halted, did not stop with this defeat.[9] We may suggest that those Huns could have been not Hephthalites but previous bands who preceded the Hephthalites. From coins we can recover the names of some of the later "Huna" rulers in the subcontinent, the two most famous of whom were Toramana and Mihrakula, ruling in the first half of the sixth century. They probably were Hephthalites, or at least in some manner connected with them.

At the same time, other Hephthalite rulers were found in northwest India and south of the Hindukush. Coins with the names of Khingila, Narendra, and others indicate continued rule of Hephthalite rulers after the defeat of their northern brethren at the hands of the Sasanians and Turks, which occurred a short time after 557, when Persians and Turks agreed to attack the Hephthalites and divide their territory between them. On the basis of coins J. Harmatta reconstructed a possible sequence of Hephthalite rulers north of the Hindukush from the middle of the fifth century to about 565 as follows (the names all end in -o which also may be read as -a): Adomano, followed by Khingila, then Alkhano I (a ruler or a tribal name), Zabolo; Meo; another Alkhano II; and Aldano. This unpublished hypothetical reconstruction, on the basis of coins, contains no names which are found in Arabic or Persian literary sources, such as Akhshunvar (or -dar, perhaps a title), Barmudha, Khushnavaz, or Katulphos in Menander's Byzantine history. Without further information, any reconstruction of the sequence of Hephthalite rulers remains subjective, and instead we should turn to events between the Sasanians and Hephthalites.

Yazdgird II (439–57) fought against the Hephthalites, and his successor Peroz (459–84) at first sought aid from them in his struggle against his brother Hormizd III, but after ascending the throne he fought and was defeated and captured by them about 469. After being released on payment of tribute, and leaving his son Kavad as a hostage until the tribute was paid, he lost his life fighting against the Hephthalites in 484. Many coins of Peroz, counterstruck with an Hephthalite sign, have been found in excavations in Central Asia, testimony to the large amount of tribute paid by the Sasanians. The payment of tribute was continued under Valash or Balash, brother of Peroz, who only ruled four years, when he was deposed by the Sasanian nobility who put Kavad on the throne.

Kavad (488–496) remained on good terms with the Hephthalites and when he was overthrown took refuge with them. With their help, especially one of their tribes, the Kadish or Kadiseni of Byzantine writings, Kavad was able to regain his throne, and he remained in their debt throughout his reign. With his son and successor Chosroes I, however, the situation changed, but only with the appearance in Transoxiana of a new group of nomads—the Turks—was the power of the Hephthalites broken by joint action of Iranians and Turks.

About 552 the empire of the Jouan-jouan was taken over by their vassals the Turks, whose center was in the Altai Mountains. Soon the Turks extended their own sway over neighboring tribes in Mongolia and the western steppes, and established a large empire. Under Ishtemi, one of the Turk leaders, an army came south and defeated the main Hephthalite force. The Sasanians acted in conjunction with the Turks and divided the Hephthalite domains, the Turks assuming rule over the lands to the north of the Oxus River and the Persians the south. This by no means meant an end to the Hephthalites, for many of their local rulers recognized the hegemony of either the Iranians or the Turks but retained their positions. In fact the Hephthalites continued to fight against one or the other of their overlords with some success. Towards the end of the reign of Hormizd IV (579–590), a prominent Iranian general, Bahram Chobin, defeated a combined Turkish-Hephthalite army near Herat. Later he revolted against his sovereign and assumed the throne for a short time. Forced to flee, he took refuge with the Hephthalites where he later was killed. Under Chosroes II (591–628), however, the attention of the Sasanians was directed towards the Byzantine Empire and the east remained quiet.

The Turks had not been idle in international relations, for they established contacts with Constantinople beginning in 563. At that time Ishtemi was one ruler of the western part of the vast domains of the Turks. Another leader was called Silziboulos, who dealt with the Byzantines. One of the issues which concerned both states was the flight of the Avars, another nomadic people, who had been under Joun-jouan and then possibly Hephthalite rule, to the west. The Byzantine historian Menander Protektor (fragments 18–23 M) gives a detailed account of an embassy sent from Constantinople to the Turks in 568 and its return. The commercial object of this and later embassies was to circumvent the Sasanians and bring silk over the steppe route to the Byzantine Empire.

The succession of Turkish supreme rulers is now known thanks to an inscription at Bugut in Mongolia.[10] Bumin, the founder of the empire and great *kaghan*, was followed by his second son Muhan who ruled from 553–572, and then was succeeded by his brother Taspar (572–581). At the death of the last, a dispute occurred in the succession, and another chief Nivar (581–587) became *kaghan*. He was faced with a rebellion in the western part of his domains. A certain Apa *kaghan* established a break-away western Turkish state, but he did not last long, and after an uncertain time we hear of a union of the Tarim Basin, Ferghana and other lands of the west, under a ruler known only in Chinese sources as T'ung *kaghan* of the western Turks, who ruled from 619 to 630, when he was murdered. Consequently the west Turkish state disintegrated, and various tribal chiefs assumed local rule until the coming of the Arabs, and the expansion into Central Asia of the T'ang dynasty of China.

What was the situation in Central Asia at the end of the seventh century before the coming of the Arabs and the Chinese revival? How had it changed from earlier times? In Mongolia and the western steppes various tribes of nomads had moved westward, but the Turks had absorbed many tribes, and had extended their rule over the Tarim basin and all of Transoxiana. Turkish chiefs had even penetrated into the mountains of present Afghanistan, but Bactria, both north and south of the Oxus, was considered outside of the hegemony of the west Turkish state, whose boundary in the south was considered to be the "Iron Gate" in the Hissar range. Bands of Turkish and other nomads, however, were to be found south of the Hissar Mountains.

Only gradually did the general designation "Turk" replace that of "Hun" and "Hephthalite," so that we are uncertain whether a ruler can be called a Turk or otherwise. On the whole, the settled population of the areas under control of Turkish rulers remained Iranian in speech. Because of the expansion of Sogdian colonies in the Chu and Ili valleys, as well as trading stations into China and Mongolia, the influence of Sogdian civilization was strong among the Turks.

In Bactria, Sogdian culture vied with Sasanian cultural strands, both of them absorbing the native traditions of the Kushans. The Khwarazmians were closely allied to the Sogdians, and by this time their merchants were extending their influence northwest to the Volga and farther. I believe by this time we can speak of a distinctive Central Asian civilization, principally Sogdian, but with other manifestations in Bactria and in the oases of eastern Turkestan. How can we characterize this culture? This will be discussed in Chapter 13.

# Notes

1. For bibliographies on the nomadic movements of this period see chs. 6 and 7 of D. Sinor, ed., *The Cambridge History of Early Inner Asia*. For eastern Turkestan cf. the bibliography in L. Hambis, ed., *L'Asie Centrale,* especially for archaeological expeditions in that region. The five volumes of F. Altheim, *Geschichte der Hunnen* (Berlin: De Gruyter, 1959–62) contain nuggets of information but must be used with great caution. The same applies to R. Ghirshman, *Les Chionites-Hephtalites,* Mémoires de la Délégation Française en Afghanistan 13 (Cairo: L'Institut Français d'Archéologie Orientale, 1948).
2. On the many forms of the name "Hun" cf. H.W. Bailey, "Harahuna," in *Asiatica, Festschrift Friedrich Weller* (Leipzig: Harrasowitz, 1954), 12–21.
3. For numismatics of Central Asia at this period cf. D.W. MacDowall, "The Monetary Systems and Currency of Central Asia," in J. Harmatta, *Prolegomena to the Sources on the History of pre-Islamic Central Asia* (Budapest: Akademiai Kiado, 1979), 307–17. On the Kushano-Sasanians see J. Cribb, "Numismatic Evidence for Kushano-Sasanian Chronology," *Studia Iranica* 19 (1990), 151–93.
4. On Alkhon cf. R. Göbl, *Dokumente,* vol. 2, index. For *war* and *warz* see W. Haussig, "Theophylakts Exkurs über die Skythischen Völker," *Byzantion* 33 (Brussels, 1954), *passim*.
5. As an example of the manner in which specialists on ancient Central Asia do their work, a detail which I noticed when in the museum of Opal, presumed birthplace of Mahmud al-Kashgari, author of the *Divan Lughat al-Turk*, may be mentioned. I recognized an unusual headdress on a ruler portrayed on a large clay sealing of a pot as identical with that on coins of a ruler of Ustrushana (see O. Smirnova, *Svodnyi Katalog Sogdiiskikh*

*Monet*, op. cit., 334). Since both objects came from archaeological levels of the same time (late 6th or early 7th century), one must then speculate whether one person is intended, or if there is a family connection between the rulers of Opal and Ustrushana. Also the question arises whether the person represented was a Hephthalite (most likely) or a Turk.

6. The coinage of Central Asia has been studied by E. Zeimal and E. Rtveladze. See the book in Russian and English by Rtveladze, ed., *Drevnie Monety Srednei Azii* (Tashkent: Izdatel'stvo literatury i iskusstva imena Gafura Gulyama, 1987).

7. On skull deformation see R. Frye, *The History of Ancient Iran*, op. cit., 350, for references, and F. Altheim, *Geschichte der Hunnen,* vol. 1, 77, but especially R. Göbl, *Dokumente,* vol. 2, 232–246. For polyandry see the discussion with references in R. Ghirshman, *Les Chionites-Hephtalites*, 125–28.

8. K. Enoki, "On the Nationality of the Ephthalites," *Memoirs of the Research Department of the Toyo Bunko* 18 (Tokyo, 1959), 1–58, supports the Badakhshan origin. On the controversy see L.N. Gumilev, "Eftality-Gortsy ili Stepyanki?" (Hephthalite mountaineers or steppe people?), in *Vestnik Drevnei Istorii* 3 (Moscow, 1967), 91.

9. On the Huns in India cf. A. Biswas, *The Political History of the Hunas in India* (Delhi: Munshiram Manoharlal, 1973), 243 pp.

10. On the inscription of Bugut, cf. S. Klyashtorny and V.A. Livshits, "The Sogdian Inscription of Bugut Revised," *Acta Orientalia Hungarica* 26 (1972), 69–102.

# CHAPTER 13

# The Merchant World
# of the Sogdians

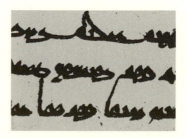

In Central Asia of the seventh century, Sogdiana was more oriented towards trade and handicraft production, while Bactria was more agricultural, similar to present northern Tajikistan contrasted with the agricultural southern part of the country. Sogdiana and Khwarazm also were more urbanized than Bactria, which more resembled Sasanian Iran in the number of *kushks* or castles, around which villages were clustered. So the civilization of Central Asia at this time may be characterized as a combination of a feudal and a merchant society.

One could speak of imperial Kushans but not of imperial Sogdians, for the latter, as far as we know, never created a large, centralized state in Central Asia. Their political organization has been characterized as similar to the ancient Greek city states, and this is valid, but the power and influence of the landed aristocracy in their fortified villas cannot be disregarded. In Sasanian Iran merchants were not highly regarded and the feudal lords monopolized power and influence, both on the land and at court. In Central Asia, on the other hand, merchants, and possibly to a certain extent heads of guilds of craftsmen, approached the landlords in power and influence, and certainly in wealth. The houses of merchants in Panjikant, Samarkand, and elsewhere were spacious, decorated with wall paintings, and in general displayed an opulence unexpected for inhabitants of small cities.

Since the major external market, as well as source of luxury goods, for the Sogdians was China, we hear in Chinese sources of embassies from Sogdiana and other lands of the west from early times, but by 600 their number was far greater than earlier. For the Central Asians the embassies, on the whole, were really trading missions, and we have mentioned the early letters in the Sogdian language from a watch

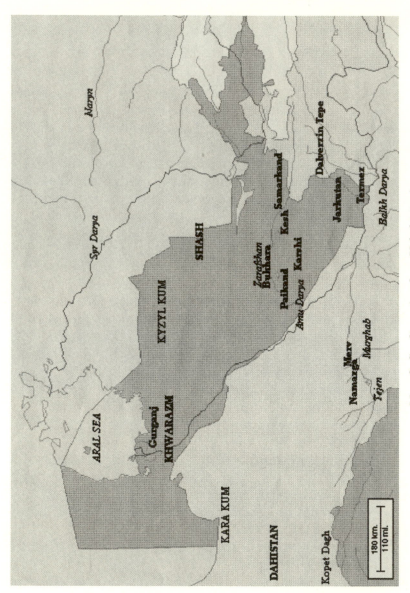

*Map G.* Sogdiana (modern Uzbekistan)

tower at the western end of the complex of walls known as the Great Wall of China dating from about 311 of our era. By that time trading colonies of Sogdians had been established far and wide, even in some regions of interior China. What was being traded?[1]

The Sogdians were great purveyors of various gems, according to Chinese tales, while Khotan was an important source of jade. Pearls and other precious stones were frequent objects of the China trade. But apart from gems, spices, ivory and manufactured objects of silver and gold, slaves were valuable commodities everywhere sought by anyone who could afford them. Musicians and dancers from Samarkand, Kucha, and elsewhere in the west were also in great demand at the Chinese courts, and of course horses were sought from nomads. Although silk dominated the textile industry of China, other cloths and woolen garments from Central Asia were brought to China. But trade was not simply in one direction, even though the riches of China attracted merchants from distant lands. All kinds of exotic animals, birds, plants, fruits or whatever, were traded and transported to whomever would pay the highest price for them. Amber, furs and honey from north Russia and the Baltic were bartered and sold in the market places of Central Asia, frequently only in transit to rich settled areas, but also to satisfy local aristocrats. International trade was in full swing by 600 and the Sogdians were well located to profit from the expansion of trade.

The abundance of copper coinage for local use is an indication of flourishing economic conditions, for silver, and rarer gold, coins were weighed for their metal content, whereas the copper coinage was used as modern coinage is. In Sogdiana we find a variety of coins from this period, and in several local Transoxian coinages it is fascinating to see the copying of Chinese style coins, with a square hole in the middle but with Sogdian legends. Whether these copper coins were then used locally as the similar Chinese coins were is uncertain. Localities under Chinese rule were forced to employ copper coins by the government, which backed the value of these, the only official coinage permitted. Because

187

the purity of Sasanian silver coins was maintained through-out the length of the dynasty, except for several short instances of deliberate debasement, they were exchanged for legal tender throughout Chinese-controlled Central Asia. What this means is that when foreign merchants came to Turfan, for example, they were forced to exchange their silver coins for local copper coins, which alone were accepted in the bazaar. The Sasanian coins probably were weighed and then exchanged for an equivalent amount of the value of the silver in local copper or bronze coins.

Beginning with the reign of Chosroes I, the Sasanians became more involved in commerce with South Arabia, India and the far East, and the government apparently was intelli-gent enough to realize the advantages of maintaining a high standard of coinage in trade, especially with foreigners.[2] Local silver coinages of the oasis states of the west not under Chinese control, such as Bukhara and Samarkand, frequent-ly were debased and not accepted as readily as Sasanian coins. See the appendix on coinages of Central Asia.

When we turn to religion, Central Asia was different from Sasanian Iran, where Christianity had made great strides in conversions by 600, while the Zoroastrian state church had become frozen with many rituals. The kind of centralized and hierarchical church found in Iran, of course, did not exist in Central Asia, where a tolerance of many religions was cou-pled with a native, local Zoroastrianism. If one wished to draw a parallel, the late Roman Empire before Constantine might provide a basis for comparison. In both, aside from the adherents of universal religions such as Christianity, Judaism and Manichaeism, there was a general respect for the local pantheon of gods and goddesses. But certain tute-lary deities in certain localities would receive special worship from the local inhabitants. It is possible that in some cases in Central Asia a private cult of a local ruler might assume the proportions of a state cult, such as the cult of the Roman emperors in Rome. From inscriptions and representations on wall paintings, we find features of both Zoroastrian and oth-er religions in the spiritual milieu of Central Asia.

In this book we take the various features of Zoroastrian-

*Figure 16.* Sogdian clay ossuary in Hermitage Museum, 6th–7th cent.

ism as found in Sasanian Iran, and among contemporary adherents of that faith, as normative for the religion. Deviations from, as well as conformity to, the norms existed in Central Asia. The holidays, many rituals, and a cult of the souls of ancestors (*fravashis*) were common to both Iran and Central Asia. Non-Zoroastrian elements in Central Asia include many clay or wood statuettes, which have been found in excavations. They have different styles, indicating various schools of glyptic art, and are not Buddhist figures. Perhaps they were related somehow to an ancient cult of the mother goddess, since so many are obvious female figurines. These votive objects of folk belief have not been found in Iran, and their significance in Central Asian religious beliefs is unclear.

Another difference between Central Asia and Iran is the extensive use of much-decorated ossuaries, which have been found all over Central Asia, but much less in Iran where decorations on them are missing. In some regions of Central Asia, there may even have been festivals connected with a cult of ossuaries. Many of the representations on the ossuaries, carved or painted, as well as those on the wall paintings, betray non-Zoroastrian appearances. In Panjikant, for example, a goddess with four arms shows Indian influence, while other representations, such as the goddess Nana on a lion, are not Iranian Zoroastrian. Nana was depicted on the coins of the Saka rulers of India, for example Azes, on Kushan coins, and in Central Asia in various poses. In Iran, on the contrary, an iconoclasm dominated the Zoroastrian religion at the end of the empire, but even here we should not assume that everyone in Iran adhered to the rules and canons of the state supported church. Unfortunately, we have no remains of wall paintings from this period in Iran, and other examples of religious art are uncertain.

In Central Asia there seems to have been a widespread cult of lamentation for the dead, where the mourners were expected to cut their faces with knives, reminiscent of the Ashura ceremony of Shiite Iran. But the same practice is reported at the funeral of Attila the Hun and other nomadic rulers, so it may have been a borrowing from nomads. The latter followed forms of shamanism and maintained similar religious beliefs after they had settled, and their influence on the settled populations cannot be excluded as a possibility. Likewise, on wall paintings when a worshipper is portrayed facing a fire altar, frequently he is shown sitting on his heels much as Persians used to sit before modern times. Such a pose, as far as we know, is not found in Iranian Zoroastrianism. It is interesting that the Old Persian word found in inscriptions for a god, *baga,* also appears in Central Asia, whereas in Sasanian Iran the word had been replaced by *yazata* or *yazd.* The significance of this difference is difficult to establish, but at least we can recognize that Central Asian Zoroastrianism was far from identical with Sasanian Zoroastrianism.

From wall paintings in many houses in Panjikant, it would seem that each family had its own patron deities. Likewise the rivers, mountains, large trees and other natural features were inhabited by spirits if not special deities, but this form of popular religion is found in many lands. In addition, there were Sogdian Christians, mostly of the Nestorian persuasion, and Manichaeans, but Buddhism apparently never attained the popularity it had in Bactria and elsewhere in Central Asia. When the Chinese Buddhist pilgrim Hsüan-tsang visited Central Asia he remarked on the scarcity of Buddhist monasteries in Samarkand, and elsewhere in Sogdiana. This is confirmed by archeology which has failed to discover characteristic *stupas* and monastery ruins in the

190

region of ancient Sogdiana. Perhaps Buddhism failed to attract the pragmatic, prosperous merchants of Sogdiana, for any political reason behind this phenomenon cannot be detected.

Although the Sogdians at home were not partial to Buddhism, in their colonies in the east they did accept Buddhism, to judge from the Sogdian translations of Buddhist books, principally from Chinese. There are two explanations for this apparent difference from the homeland. First, the Sogdians may have sought to please their Buddhist, Chinese and other customers, by patronizing the translations of Buddhist texts into Sogdian, without themselves thereby seeking to disseminate Buddhism. On the other hand, if they had become fervent followers of the Buddha and wished to acquire merit by the translations, the best and most complete versions of the Buddhist works at that time (seventh and later centuries) were probably only to be found in China, where competent monks had long ago systematically translated the Buddhist books into Chinese. It is a good surmise that by the time when the translations into Sogdian were made, the Tokharian, Khotanese, or even Sanskrit versions of Buddhist works were incomplete or defective, and only in China were authoritative translations at hand. In any case, the Sogdian translations of Buddhist works do not indicate a mass conversion of Sogdians to Buddhism even in the eastern colonies, for translations into Sogdian of Christian and Manichaean religious writings also have been found. Furthermore, those translations are late in date, after the seventh century. We may conjecture that on the whole the Sogdians held to their national religious practices and beliefs, which as mentioned, were not the same as those of the Zoroastrians of Iran.

The folklore of Central Asia also shows differences from Iran. In the latter we find many stories relating to rulers, such as the tale of Chosroes and Shirin, or the exploits of Bahram Gor. In Central Asia, on the other hand, apparently there were several strands, the most prominent being the Saka epic cycle of Rustam and his deeds. Regardless whether much of what he did was copied from the feats of Greek

Heracles, the Sakas had many stories which were incorporated in the work of Firdosi, who finished his "Book of Kings" in the eleventh century. Parthian minstrels probably contributed much to the dissemination of the Saka cycle in the west.

Another epic cycle seems to have been that principally of the Sogdians, with their hero Siyavush, for in pre-Islamic Bukhara his death was remembered in song and story.[3] All of these strands came together in what may be called an all-Iranian national epic, best known from Firdosi's book, although others existed which have not survived. The elements of myth, folklore, religion and history are all to be found in this all-Iranian epic, about which much has been written.[4] Here only the contrast between the more prosaic stories of Iran, with the folkloric and poetic epics of Central Asia needed to be mentioned. The antiquated view of Central Asia as a provincial extension of Sasanian Iran even in this domain is shown to be false.

The most spectacular aspect of Central Asian society is found in the fine arts, the vestiges of which have remained down to the present, especially in the oasis sites of eastern Central Asia. A general characterization of the nature of Central Asian art could be that it was secular, as contrasted with Indian art which was predominantly religious, while Sasanian art was imperial. The art of Central Asia, as seen primarily in the wall paintings, was devoted to epic themes and stories, and representations of the aristocracy, although figures of deities, of course, were not absent. The splendid costumes worn by aristocrats in the wall paintings of Varakhsha, Samarkand, Panjikant, Qyzyl, Bezeklik and Tunhuang, to mention only a few outstanding sites, rivaled the brocades and velvets of Medieval European knights and their ladies. The parallel of Central Asia at this time with northern Europe, and its trading cities beside the manors of knights, is striking. Although I have put together the art of eastern and western Central Asia, of Panjikant and Kucha for example, this does not mean that there were no differences, but the society which is represented in the arts is the same.

The various schools of Central Asian art in the few centuries before the Arab conquests have been studied by many
scholars and show, as one would expect, Sasanian motifs and
influences in the western Central Asian sites and Chinese
motifs and influences in the eastern art specimens found in
Tun-huang and other places. In my opinion, what we find at
this time in Central Asia is a flowering of a civilization which
is not provincial Sasanian or Chinese, but independent in its
own right, and this is best seen in the fine arts. It is not possible, however, to discuss the many aspects of art in Central
Asia, which has been done by others.[5]

To return to more mundane subjects, which perhaps
would have occupied the attention of a trading people more
than affairs of the spirit, in what respect did social structure,
land ownership, and such matters in Central Asia differ from
those in Iran? Perhaps the most striking difference in society
between the two was the mixture of social structure with
official positions at court, or in the administration, in Iran,
and the more simplified formation in Central Asia. In
Sasanian Iran, with a centralized court of the king-of-kings,
society was stratified in an almost caste-like structure.
According to ancient religious principles society was divided
into three classes: the nobility, members of the religious institution, and the common folk, both artisans and peasants. The
nobility was further differentiated between the local kings or
rulers *(shahrdaran)*, members of the royal family
*(vaspuhrakan)*, the great feudal lords *(wuzurgan)*, and the
lower nobility *(azatan)*. The great feudal lords were the leaders of prominent families, with extensive land holdings such
as the Suren and Karen families, while the lower nobility was
formed by knights or what are called *dihqans* in the sources.
This picture was complicated by an uncertain placing of
members of the administration, bureaucracy, or army, such
as generals and court officials, in the strata of society.
Usually high offices were held by members of the aristocracy,
but at times the ranks became confused, although protocol
was very important at that time. By the end of the Sasanian
Empire we find a fourth class—the scribes or bureaucrats—
acknowledged as important in society. The almost rigid

*Figure 17.* Panjikant, burnt wooden panel,
hero fighting monster, 7th cent.

stratification of society is mentioned in many sources.

In Central Asia, as we learn from Sogdian letters from
Mt. Mugh, the social situation was much simpler.6 To begin,
the ruler of a city state, such as Bukhara or Samarkand, did
not have anything like the standing of the emperor of
Sasanian Iran. Rather the local ruler was a primus inter
pares of the local nobility, which was not stratified as in Iran.
Society in Sogdiana was divided into three classes: the nobility (''ztk'r), merchants (γ w'kr), and workers or ordinary folk
(k'rykr). The local ruler from among the nobility had different

194

titles in different areas, such as Afshin in Ustrushana, Ikhshid in Samarkand, etc. The notable absence in Central Asia is the organization of priests, which in Iran was divided into a hierarchy of chief mobad, lower ranks of mobads, herbads, rads (a judicial office), and others, in a kind of parallel to the secular ranks. Zoroastrian priests, of course, existed in Central Asia, but without the status of officials of a state religion, the priests of Central Asian Zoroastrianism seem to have had little difference in standing from the religious leaders of Christianity or Manichaeism.

In both Iran and Central Asia commercial law and family law were similar, and from marriage contracts in Central Asia and Middle Persian texts from Iran dealing with such affairs, we see that in both lands polygamy was practiced, including a principal wife and subordinate spouses. Slavery also existed in both lands, and slaves were not considered as part of the structure of society in either Iran or Central Asia. Most slaves were domestic slaves, and were secured by purchase, although prisoners of war could be sold into slavery. Although slaves did till the land, on the whole they were not as efficient as free laborers who were in the great majority. Furthermore, the peasant usually was part of a village commune, but not like the serf of Medieval Europe who was bound to the land. The presence of nomads nearby, the existence of many towns, and the lack of a centralized empire or kingdom in Central Asia, made it possible for the peasant to flee from inordinate demands or taxes, although in practice the peasant rarely left his village. It also should be noted that there is no evidence in Iran or Central Asia of a system of mutual obligations between lord and underling, as in Europe in degrees from the top down to the serf. We do not find mutual obligations or interactions, other than financial, between members of classes in Central Asia and Iran.

At the same time there was an institution peculiar to Central Asia, especially in Sogdiana, that of the *chakar*, which in the Central Asian context might be translated as military slave or *mameluke* but which in modern Persian simply means "servant." In my opinion later institutions, such as the Janissaries of the Ottoman Empire and the

Mamelukes of Egypt, had their origin in this Central Asian practice of purchasing slaves and training them to be guards of the homes of merchants, who departed on long voyages to China and elsewhere. These slaves soon developed into private armies of rich merchants or landowners beholden to their masters. This practice spread in Islamic times to the 'Abbasid caliphate and to the court of the Samanids in Bukhara, followed by the Ghaznavids and later dynasties.

Land in this part of the world is worthless without water, which means irrigation, and this implies local organization, and a chief in a village. Theoretically all land in Iran belonged to the ruler, i.e. the state, and he could assign it to whomever he pleased, which was not the case in Central Asia. In actuality, land and villages in both lands were bought and sold to whomsoever had the resources to buy them. Peasants were subject to corvée (forced labor), and their working day was supposed to be divided into three parts, one part for the ruler or owner, another part for maintenance and purchase of seed, needs of the peasant, etc., while a third part may have belonged to the village, although the destination of the proceeds in the division remains unclear. The unit of taxation was not the individual but the whole village, and taxes were paid in kind, for money seems to have been used mainly in towns with markets. Much is unclear at the local level since documentation is lacking, but conditions in villages in Central Asia seem to have been much like those in Iran.

Already in the pre-Islamic period, bazaars existed in Central Asian towns, with many of later characteristics of Islamic times, including caravanserais, warehouses in the bazaars, and shops where craftsmen plied their wares, both making and selling them. Partnerships in trade, both local and long distance, were formed and the economy flourished. Certain towns became famous for specialties. For example, the town of Zandana in the oasis of Bukhara was famous for a richly woven cloth, which continued to enjoy a high reputation in Islamic times. Clothes were beautifully decorated, as can be seen on the wall paintings in Panjikant, Samarkand and Varakhsha. It should be noted that the thriving economy was not limited to a few large centers, but small towns and villages partook of the riches from trade. The Sogdian merchants were adept in dealing with the nomads, and much of their success came from cooperation with the political powers who ruled the steppes and even their own oases. The nomads, inclined to extortion from, or protection of, settled communities, found it to their advantage to use Sogdian merchants as their intermediaries in international trade. Inasmuch as the nomads feared no political domination by the Sogdians they became their partners, while the Chinese merchants were not trusted because of the political ambitions of their rulers. One could almost say that in Central Asia the Chinese thought politically while the Sogdians thought economically.

Such, in brief, was the civilization of the Central Asians. By 600 the importance of the Sogdians had grown, to the extent that their language had become a *lingua franca* for all of Central Asia. The various oasis city states not only flourished, even while subject to nomadic rulers, but gradually began to cooperate rather than only compete in trading.

But everything was to change with the coming of a new force which was to alter the face not only of Iran and Central Asia but of much of Asia and Africa. This was the greatest upheaval ever experienced by those regions, more than Hellenism, and until the present, even of Westernization. It was the religion of Islam, borne by the Arabs, but adopted frequently with fanatical zeal by those who were conquered. Not just a religion, but a way of life and a new society, was the message brought by Islam, and so it happened.

# Notes

1. The standard works on articles of trade are B. Laufer, *Sino-Iranica* (Chicago: Field Museum, 1919), and E. Schafer, *The Golden Peaches of Samarkand* (Berkeley: Univ. of California Press, 1963).
2. Cf. R. Frye, "Sasanian-Central Asian Trade Relations," *Bulletin of the Asia Institute* 7 (1993), 73–77.
3. On Siyavush cf. G. Azarpay, *Sogdian Painting* (Berkeley: Univ. of California Press, 1981), 128–132.

4. For the Iranian epic see O. Davidson, *Poet and Hero in the Persian Book of Kings* (Ithaca: Cornell Univ. Press, 1994), with bibliography.
5. On the art of Central Asia see Azarpay, op. cit., and many books of Galina Pugachenkova such as *Ocherki Iskusstva Srednei Azii* (Moscow: Isskustvo, 1982).
6. The Mugh documents have been published in a series called *Sogdiiskie Dokumenty s gory Mug*: vol. 2, by V.A. Livshits, on juridical documents and letters (Moscow, 1962), and vol. 3, by O. Smirnova and M. Bogolyubov, on economic documents (Moscow, 1963). Also important is O. Smirnova, *Ocherki iz istorii Sogda* (Moscow: Nauka, 1970).

# CHAPTER 14

# Caliphs and Kaghans

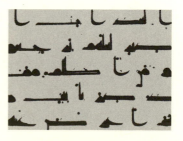

Whereas in the pre-Islamic period of the history of Central Asia we were plagued with a lack of written materials, most of which were religious, now an avalanche of sources descends on the scene.[1] Historiography changes from wringing the most information possible out of a word or an art object, with a great measure of subjective interpretation, to the task in the Islamic period of comparing different versions of reported events, with the aim of determining which is reliable and why. Numismatics loses its paramount role in chronology, art history and religion, and is relegated to determining the exact dates of a ruler over certain territories. Art objects too lose their great importance in determining features of society and even culture. In short, the entire approach to the history of Central Asia changes, which is why few scholars have ventured to cross the chasm between ancient and Islamic history, and they almost seem to follow a pattern of the adherents of universal religions, in deciding that real history begins with whatever period concerns them. Yet such momentous changes as those between Islam and what Muslim authors call the previous age of ignorance did not happen over night. How did the pre-Islamic civilization of Central Asia respond to the Arabs with their religion?

It has been said that fanatics make history, but they are many times the first to die in battle for their fanaticism. This may have been true of Muslims, for certainly the speed with which they overthrew the Sasanian Empire, and much of the Byzantine Empire, left the impression in Europe, enhanced by the Crusades, that the Arabs came from the desert with the Qur'an in one hand and a sword in the other, with the message "convert or be killed." Actually that was far from the truth, for at first Islam was held to be a religion for the Arabs alone, or also for their clients. When the Bedouin tribes accepted Islam and defeated the Sasanian and Byzantine armies, they did what they had always done in Arabia, accepted the defeated into their tribes as clients (*mawali*). The latter frequently were invited to accept Islam if there was mutual agreement in joining the tribe. Also in Arabia the result of victory had been booty, so at least for the tribes the Islamic conquests were great expeditions for riches. So the real message of the Muslim armies to opponents or to besieged towns was "pay tribute or fight." Both Iran and Central Asia had long experience in paying tribute to nomadic raiders and, although the new invaders came from the south and west, for the most part they were met with payment of tribute, similar to previous nomadic invaders from the depths of Inner Asia.

But the Arabs, after initial contacts, changed from mere raiders to conquerors, who intended to occupy the rich lands they had conquered. There are many reasons for their successes, but the power of a new religion, which after the conquest of Iran had already slowly begun to evolve from an Arab one to a universal one, cannot be underestimated. The Arabs themselves, like the Christians and Manichaeans, vacillated between exclusivity of their religion and the desire for universality. At times, especially during the Umayyad Caliphate, prospective converts were refused acceptance into the religion, usually because they would attain the benefits of being a Muslim, which included a remission of paying the head or poll tax, and even in some instances the land tax. Revenues to the state, however, took precedence over any religious exigencies. Throughout pre-Islamic history in China and the Near East, including Iran, the state or the ruler generally held primacy over religious leaders. In the Central Asian oasis states, however, the ruler frequently paid homage to the holy person of a religion, and this attitude may have originated in Buddhism or in shamanism for the nomads. But this is another subject.

The Central Asians at first regarded the Arabs much as they had past nomadic invaders; they should be accepted for their military prowess, obeyed, bribed, and then, if they settled down, absorbed. The early raids of the Arabs seemed to be a repetition of past encounters with Huns and Turks. But the Arab forces were different in several respects. First, the Bedouin tribes had a stamina, born from the desert sands, even greater than that of the northern nomads. Second, they had incorporated into their armies well-trained, professional soldiers of the Sasanian Empire, whom they had conquered. How many of these former soldiers joined the Arab tribes is unknown, but in the conquests in Iraq and Iran the sources tell us of units of the Sasanian army joining the Arabs, after seeing that their government had collapsed. This means that the Arab armies included not only experienced cavalry, but also engineers conversant with sieges. Third, and most important, the Arabs brought not only a new religion, but also a social message of equality, the end of classes, and the solidarity of belonging together in a great family of Muslims, the *ummah*. In the division of booty some tribal chiefs at times neglected to give the clients of the tribe an equal share, which caused resentment and even conflict. On the whole, however, clients were considered members of the tribe to be rewarded for their prowess in battle as any of the Bedouin. When non-Arabs converted to Islam they were given Arabic names and, according to our sources, they were said to have become Arabs. As frequently happens with new converts, many became more fanatic than the Arabs.

In the conquest of Iran the Arabs, with an ever growing number of clients in their armies, followed the time-honored path of Alexander along the main trade route to the east. The deserts did not hinder the Arabs but may even have attracted them, which would explain why Qum, on the edge of the Kavir, was settled by the Arabs, and became a base for further expansion. The Arabs took more time to reach Merv than it had Alexander to reach Central Asia, but then they were not driven by a single-minded ruler. Just as Alexander had been concerned about the possibility of resistance by the last Achaemenid king in the eastern part of his domains, so the Arabs also were worried about the last Sasanian ruler Yazdgird III. When he was killed in the oasis of Merv in 651 by a miller, the Sasanian Empire was definitely ended and a new regime took over the administration of the new domains.

In place of the king of kings, a caliph, successor of the prophet Muhammad, became ruler of a vast empire, but it was unlike previous empires, for the early caliphs had no royal court with a bureaucracy to administer the newly conquered lands. They had to rely on the previous administrations and bureaucracies to collect taxes and keep order. There must have been a period of chaos in changing from an old to a new regime, but evidence shows that on the local level very little was changed. In Iran the top echelons of church and state were removed or fled, but the structures underneath remained, especially in villages and in entire regions, such as Azerbaijan and Fars, where the Arabs did not settle in any numbers. The Caspian provinces, the central deserts and Baluchistan were hardly noticed by the Arabs. The trade route to the east, through Khurasan, was important and had to be controlled by the Arabs, with garrisons and settlements.

The first contacts of the Muslim forces with Central Asia, at the time of the first caliphs ruling from Arabia, were raids into Bactria, called by the Arabs Tokharistan, after the tribe of the Kushan Empire that had settled there. Even though the Arabs may have reached Balkh, there was at that time no occupation of lands in the large eastern province of the Sasanian Empire called Khurasan.

Although a treaty was concluded by the Arabs with the local ruler of Merv, Mahoye, who had the title "warden of the marches" (*marzban*) about 656, there is no evidence at that time that the Arabs settled in the oasis, although possibly some did. It was not until the Umayyad Caliphate was established in Damascus that yearly raids became permanent occupation, and just as Merv had been the Sasanian base for defense and operations in the east, so it now became the same for the Arabs. In this respect it paralleled Basra and Kufa in Mesopotamia, which were the two centers of the viceroy of the eastern part of the Umayyad Caliphate, from which troops were sent to the east. The settlement in Merv, however, was unlike Basra and Kufa, which were new foundations for the sole purpose of permanently housing the Muslim Arab warriors, apart from the local population. In

Merv the Arabs were settled among the local population, and this contributed to a policy of assimilation, which took place in Khurasan more and sooner than in Iraq and Iran.

The Arab tribes were the real power in the east throughout the Umayyad Caliphate, and they were settled in Merv along tribal lines. Damascus, the Umayyad capital, sought to centralize tax collecting, and the payment of pensions to the warriors of the tribes in the hands of officials sent from Damascus, instead of following the practice of the tribal chiefs controlling both functions. In this the caliph was only partially successful, for the chiefs frequently usurped the offices. Ancient feuds followed the settlement of tribes in Merv, as well as elsewhere in Khurasan, and tribal warfare fills the pages of the histories of Umayyad rule. The tribes were able to unite, however, in further raids for booty. But Central Asia proved as difficult a nut to crack for the Arabs as it had been for Alexander. If for so long it had not been regarded as a field for booty and exploitation for revenues, perhaps the conquest of Central Asia would have proceeded faster. As it turned out, it did not become an integral part of the Islamic world until after the establishment of the 'Abbasid Caliphate. The governors of Khurasan, under the viceroy of the caliph in Iraq, were the leaders of raids into Transoxiana.

'Ubaidallah ibn Ziyad became governor of Khurasan, the vast eastern province of the Sasanian Empire, in 673, and he was the first to lead an army across the Oxus River, called the Jaihun by the Arabs, into the oasis of Bukhara, although his father may have crossed into the oasis when he previously raided along the western bank of the river. This first real incursion of the Arabs into Sogdiana was successful, inasmuch as 'Ubaidallah obtained booty and slaves whom he took with him as a bodyguard to Basra. Legend has it that the ruler of Bukhara at that time was a woman with the title Khatun in the sources, and a number of stories circulated about her relations with the Arab leader. There probably was a queen of Bukhara, but her time of rule and actions are uncertain and local tradition exaggerated her role.

Sa'id, the son of the caliph 'Uthman, was the next governor of Khurasan, and he too raided Bukhara as well as Samarkand. His forces then raided Kesh and Termez. On his return to Arabia he also took Sogdian slaves with him to Medina where they rebelled and killed him. The death of the first Umayyad caliph Mu'awiya brought a halt to the raids, and only after suppression of the revolt of Ibn Zubair, and the death of Husain, son of the caliph 'Ali, could expeditions into Sogdiana proceed under the caliph Yazid, son and successor of Mu'awiya. In 681 he appointed Salm ibn Ziyad governor of Khurasan, and the latter not only raided Sogdiana but apparently spent the winter in Samarkand. Previously the Arabs had retreated to Merv for the winter after their raids. The Sogdians were not idle, however, and fought against the Arabs, sometimes with the help of Turkish nomads, but the Arab armies were usually victorious.

One important reason for the victory of the Muslim armies was the lack of cooperation between the various Central Asian city states, the rulers of which at times made peace with, and even joined, the Arabs. The Sogdian side of the struggle shows vacillation and changes in the policy of various groups, the merchants in search of stability and peace, but the landed nobility more belligerent. Although the merchants might cooperate among themselves, their collective did not produce leadership and it was left to the landed aristocracy to lead opposition to the Arabs. In addition to local Turkish tribes, the west Turkish state or *Kaghanate* was an important factor in the struggles against the Arabs.

The Turkish states in Mongolia and on the steppes always had a double system of sovereignty, but the succession to the prime chiefdom was lateral, from ruler to sub-ruler, rather than brother to younger brother as we find among Saka and Parthian rulers of the Indian borderlands. There was a hierarchy of ranks in the division of authority and rule over the eastern and the western (called right and left) parts of the Turkish nomadic empire. Under each *kaghan* was a corresponding *yabghu* and a *shad*; but the exact significance of these ranks is unclear. This has caused confusion in the sources, both Chinese and Arabic, in the identification of which Turkish ruler fought against the Arabs. Changes in the fortunes of various Turkish tribes also obscured identification of which Turks aided the Sogdians in their resistance to the Arabs, or who became allied with them.

At the last part of the seventh century, the power of the Turks, both in their eastern and western domains, had been checked by the Chinese, and only a few tribes near the Orkhon River were beginning to recover and form a new state, but no help could be sent to the Sogdians when they needed it. The scene was to change by the end of the century, however, with the new Turkish state, but even then several tribes of Turks, among them the Türgesh and Karluk, did not follow the authority of the Orkhon Turks, to call them after the site of their runic inscriptions.

The Sogdians, however, did not need outside help, because with the death of the caliph Yazid in 683 revolts broke out among the Arabs, and inter-tribal warfare threatened their position in Khurasan. Transoxiana, called "the other side of the river" by the Arabs, though under the governor of Khurasan, was considered a frontier area, subject to raids for plunder and booty. The revolts inside the caliphate gave Central Asia a respite from raids by the Arabs for several decades.

It should be noted that Khurasan, with Transoxiana, was not the only front on which the Arabs fought, for Sistan and the southern approaches to India were also part of the expansion in the east. In Sistan an additional problem was the gathering of Kharijites, Islamic sectarians, who did not recognize the authority of the Umayyad Caliphate, and caused much fighting for Umayyad armies. One might call this the southern front for the advances of Arab armies against mountainous principalities south of the Hindukush Mountains. Here the town of Bost, as the base of Arab operations in the south, was a parallel to Merv in Khurasan. But let us briefly look at a few events in Damascus, which had repercussions in our area, before returning to Central Asia.

The Umayyad Caliphate was beset with many troubles following the death of Yazid, for his infant son died after a few months, and tribal warfare became endemic. The complicated alliances and enmities between North Arabian and South

Arabian tribes, Qays and Kalb and others, are not our concern, except to note that the blood feuds between tribes in Syria and Iraq had their counterpart in Khurasan. In 684 Marwan, the leader of a collateral Umayyad family, was able to defeat an attempt by the Qays tribe to usurp power, and he was able to establish himself as caliph. He only lived less than a year, and his son 'Abd al-Malik succeeded him in the caliphate. But many revolts, plus war with the Byzantines, kept the new caliph from any attention to Khurasan for a number of years. Under 'Abd al-Malik, Arabic replaced Middle Persian and Greek (in the eastern and western parts of the caliphate) for administrative purposes, and new coins were struck, without the old Sasanian and Byzantine images, but with pious Arabic legends instead. Khurasan, however, was slow to accept these changes. At the end of his reign, with peace established in most of the land, the caliph turned his attention to the east. He did not live to implement a new policy in the east, but he laid the groundwork.

In 705 Walid, brother of 'Abd al-Malik, succeeded him on the caliphal throne, for that is what the caliphate had become, a change from a tribal organization to an empire. He continued the offensive policy of his brother, who had been able to restore order in Khurasan before his death. One of the rebels against the caliph 'Abd al-Malik in Khurasan was 'Abdallah ibn Khazim, a tribal leader who had created an independent following. He was finally killed by Umayyad forces, but he had sent his son Musa previously to occupy Termez, which he held for fifteen years against attacks by both Umayyad government and local forces. The chaotic situation in Khurasan was changed, however, with the appointment of Hajjaj ibn Yusuf, a strong governor or viceroy of Iraq, which, of course, included the eastern provinces. He was given almost a free hand in the entire east, and he appointed an energetic leader of the Azd tribe called Muhallab to restore order in Khurasan, which he did. The latter brought many of his tribe to Central Asia, some of whom were famous as weavers, which later became important in their cooperation with local textile workers. At the death of Muhallab in 702 his son Yazid succeeded him and raided Buttam, but he could not dislodge Musa from Termez. Hajjaj removed Yazid in 704 and appointed Yazid's brother Mufaddal as governor of Khurasan. Mufaddal was able to defeat Musa, who was killed in Termez, but Hajjaj had someone else in mind, and at the end of the same year Qutaiba ibn Muslim was appointed governor of Khurasan. A new policy was needed if Central Asia was to become part of the Umayyad Caliphate, and Qutaiba was the instrument of that policy.

Qutaiba, as a member of a small Arab tribe, did not participate in the tribal factions of Qays, Azd, Tamim, etc. in Khurasan, and this helped him to bring unity among the Arabs to continue expeditions into Central Asia. The two centers of resistance to Arab rule were Tokharistan (as we shall now call ancient Bactria) and Sogdiana, and Qutaiba moved first against Balkh. His new policy was to enlist local fighters in his army and to reconcile the local population to Arab rule, which he did with a carrot and stick approach. He was successful in restoring Arab authority in Tokharistan, leaving permanent garrisons in the cities and enlisting local leaders in his forces. One of them was Nezak, Hephthalite prince of Badghis, who accompanied Qutaiba on his expedition into Transoxiana, and whose name was really a family or tribal name, used as a title by both earlier and succeeding rulers.

The next year, 706, Qutaiba captured the important town of Paikand in the oasis of Bukhara, but when he left to return to Merv the town revolted and Qutaiba returned to sack the city, after which he massacred the male population, taking their women and children as slaves. By this he intended to send a message that revolts against Arab authority would bring swift and severe retribution. The following year Qutaiba returned to the oasis, but was unable to take Bukhara after much fighting. In 709, however, he did capture Bukhara where he now settled Arabs in the city. Tughshada, the son of Khatun, was retained as lord of Bukhara, which was a pattern now to be followed elsewhere. Tarkhun, the ruler of Samarkand, made peace with Qutaiba, paying him tribute and sending him hostages. This, however, brought about the downfall and death of Tarkhun, who was replaced by Ghurak, leader of a popular revolt. Before Qutaiba could

*Figure 18.* Wall painting of Bactrian ambassador to
Afrasiyab, Samarkand, 7th cent.
(from L.I. Albaum, Zhivopis' Afrasiyaba, Tashkent, 1975, 49)

intervene, however, he was called to Tokharistan.

Nezak had left Qutaiba, and he now incited the princes of Tokharistan to form an alliance against the Arabs. In 710 Qutaiba moved against the allies who melted away. Nezak surrendered on the promise of amnesty, but was executed by order of Hajjaj. In southern Tokharistan Qutaiba established Arab control stronger than previously. Then he crossed the Oxus and subdued the small principalities in northern Tokharistan. Afterwards he crossed the Hissar range through the "Iron Gate" and secured the submission of Kesh and Nasaf before continuing to Bukhara, where he confirmed Tughshada as ruler of the oasis and executed some of his opponents.

Qutaiba not only established permanent garrisons in the conquered cities, but built mosques and recruited local fighters into his army, which was the essence of the new policy. Because of his successes in Central Asia, he was called away from Khurasan to assist the Arab forces in Sistan in their conflict with a local ruler in southern Afghanistan called the *zunbil*. After some fighting the latter submitted, allowing Qutaiba to return to Khurasan, where he received a request from the ruler of Khwarazm for aid in restoring him to his throne, from which he had been chased by rebels. In 712 Qutaiba restored the Khwarazmshah and killed his opponents, but a further revolt in the country brought Qutaiba back, and he ravaged the land, installing an Arab governor beside the son of the Khwarazmshah who had been killed. According to the Khwarazmian scholar al-Biruni, writing in the eleventh century, Qutaiba destroyed the ancient culture of the country by killing all the learned people and destroying their writings. Both Paikand and Khwarazm were lessons for anyone who would revolt against Arab rule.

Qutaiba then turned against Samarkand, which had withheld tribute, and after many skirmishes and a siege of the city Ghurak surrendered. A strong Arab garrison was installed in the city, and Qutaiba made it the base for further operations against Shash, Khojent and Ferghana. He did not execute Ghurak, who made his peace with the Arabs, although the circumstances of his rule in Samarkand are unclear. Everywhere Qutaiba was successful, but in 714, when on a campaign in Shash, he heard of the death of his patron Hajjaj which caused him to return to Merv. Reappointed in his position, he returned to Ferghana, where news reached him of the death of Caliph Walid in 715 and the accession of the Caliph's brother Sulaiman, an enemy of Qutaiba. The latter promptly removed Qutaiba from his command, which caused him to revolt, but he was abandoned, not only by most of his Arab troops but also by local units which he had formed. He was killed and his head sent to Sulaiman, but it marked the end of Arab advances in Central Asia for many years.

Legends proliferated about Qutaiba, including a report that he had conquered Kashgar. It is possible that groups of Arabs joined local rulers as mercenaries in local struggles in Central Asia, but the Umayyad government was not involved.

While Qutaiba had such success in Central Asia, another protege of Hajjaj, Muhammad ibn al-Qasim, had secured Arab control of lands to the southeast of Sistan, including Sind and the town of Multan, where much booty was secured. But he too was removed from his office by the caliph Sulaiman, and Arab forces retreated from far conquests in that direction. The same policies of reconciliation of the local population and establishing Arab garrisons had been followed in the southeast, but now both there and in Khurasan, Arab arms suffered setbacks.

The caliph Sulaiman died in 717 and was succeeded by his cousin, the pious caliph 'Umar II, who ruled from 717 to 720. He instituted policies of conversion and of reconciliation between Arabs and their *mawali*, who had disputed the privileges pertaining to Muslims, as well as between Arabs and non-Arabs. All were now declared equal by 'Umar, and henceforth no Muslim should pay either a land or a head tax, but land was to belong to the community, and no Muslim should buy land with taxes already on it. This policy was only partially carried out, and after 'Umar's death there was a relapse on the part of the government, and also by many newly converted Muslims, especially when the Arabs returned to the harsh conduct characteristic of Qutaiba. Force, as well as reconciliation, was needed to keep the allegiance of the princes of Transoxiana to the caliphate, but there was no Qutaiba anywhere to lead the Arabs. On the other hand, Bukhara continued to be the center of Arab power in Transoxiana, as Balkh was for Tokharistan, while Arab garrisons were stationed in Samarkand and other cities. The countryside, however, remained under local control. Local princes retained their positions, but beside them were Arab tax collectors, who at times also were military leaders. Nonetheless, the position of the Arabs in Central Asia was precarious.

The Sogdian leaders hoped for aid from the Chinese and the Turks against the Arabs, but they were disappointed, so many Sogdians fled to Ferghana in 721. They were followed by the Arabs, who defeated them and executed many. Afterwards, however, the Türgesh came to the aid of the Sogdians, and for several years they controlled the countryside, although they were unable to take the walled cities. For ten years, from 728 to 738, it seemed as though the Türgesh would oust the Arabs from Transoxiana, but the death of the leader of the Turks changed the situation. At the same time his opponent, the governor of Khurasan, Asad ibn 'Abdallah, died, and was replaced by the last Umayyad governor of Khurasan, Nasr ibn Sayyar, who promoted a policy of conciliation with the local aristocracy. In spite of fluctuations in Arab policy between force and cruelty and conciliation, the latter policy was beginning to prevail, as more and more natives realized that the Arabs were here to stay, and many of the local people were becoming Muslims. When Qutaiba built a mosque in Bukhara he rewarded every local person who came to the mosque to pray on Friday. Merchants, of course, saw advantages in joining the Arabs with their far-flung caliphate, and great land owners were alternately attracted or repelled by the Umayyad government which exacted and then remitted taxes when there was danger of a revolt.

Umayyad rule in Khurasan began to experience a series of revolts by Arabs joined with *mawali*, an indication of the changed situation, which suggests one should now substitute the word Muslim for Arab. In 739 Nasr reaped the benefits of his new policy of amnesty and taxation reform for both *mawali* and the Sogdian landowners. Many of them supported him on his expeditions against Shash and Ferghana. Refugees who had fled to Ferghana were allowed to return to their homes in Sogdiana, and in general Nasr was well liked by the local population. Sogdian merchants even gave loans to the government for its expeditions, expecting rich returns from the acquisition of booty by conquests.

Nasr, like Qutaiba before him, did not belong to a power-ful Arab tribe in Khurasan. Whereas this had proven advan-tageous for Qutaiba, now it was detrimental for Nasr, who did not have a strong person like Hajjaj to aid him. It is clear that the Arab tribesmen in Khurasan overthrew Nasr and Umayyad authority, not the local population or even the *mawali,* except those still allied to the tribes.

The end of the Umayyad Caliphate also saw the end of any serious resistance to Islam in western Central Asia. It also was the end of any Chinese intervention in the west, and the last battle of Talas (or Taraz) in July 751 marks that end. Ziyad ibn Salih, lieutenant of Abu Muslim, the architect of the defeat first of Nasr ibn Sayyar and then of the Umayyads in Iraq, had suppressed a revolt in Bukhara, and then marched against a combined Chinese and Turkish army near Talas. The ruler of Shash had invaded Ferghana, whose king had called for assistance from the Chinese, while Shash allied with the Arabs. The Turks were Karluks, who had replaced the Türgesh in this part of Central Asia. At the bat-tle the Karluks deserted the Chinese, who were defeated, and many captives were brought to Samarkand, where, it is reported, they started a paper making industry.

After the battle a last feeble attempt to revolt against Islamic rule was made by the local princes, but it was sup-pressed with severity. The ruler of Kesh was killed, the lord of Bukhara, son of Tughshada, named Qutaiba after the Arab conqueror, was executed, and others lost their lives. Islam had triumphed after a half century of bitter struggle. The Tajiks, the name given to the Arabs, so-called after the Tayy tribe in Iraq, by the Sasanians and adopted by the Sogdians, came to stand for Muslims speaking any tongue, but finally it came to mean the Muslim Persian speakers of Central Asia.[2]

One interesting detail of the wars in Central Asia, between Arabs and local people, was the presence of a size-able number of refugees from Iran, who hoped to continue the struggle against the Arabs, with the help of local knights, as well as Chinese and Turkish assistance. We hear of members of the family of Yazdgird III not only soliciting aid in China, but participating in battles against the Arabs in Central Asia.

214

*Figure 19.* Central Asian silver plate of the 8th-9th cent.,
similar to Sasanian dishes
(from B.I. Marshak, Sogdiiskoe Serebro, Moscow, 1971, plate T-31)

While alliances were made and broken between various par-
ties in the Central Asian arena, the steady progress of Islam
among the populace continued.

Another process was transpiring in Central Asia, which
may be called the Persianization of the area. How did it come
to pass that the Bactrian, Khwarazmian and Sogdian languages vanished, together with their literatures and cultures, so that an all-Iranian culture and the Persian
language dominated the eastern Islamic world? There are
many reasons, one of which was the great amount of death

215

and destruction wrought by the Arab forces in Central Asia as compared with Iran. It must be remembered that in Iran a system of identity of people was based on their religion, by which internal affairs in each religious community were governed by the religious leaders of that community. This system was continued by the Muslim Arabs, even down to the Ottoman Empire with its *millet* system. This meant that the Christian and Jewish communities in Iran, with Zoroastrians now added to them, could continue their ghetto-like existence under new Arab masters, much as they had under the Sasanians. We must remember that non-Islamic peoples had community but not individual rights. In Central Asia where the majority of the people were probably local Zoroastrians, however, there was no strong religious community to hold their people together in the face of Islamic conversion. The much greater amount of fighting in Central Asia, as compared with Iran, also destroyed the links holding people together, so that when the intellectuals of Khwarazm were killed during Qutaiba's invasion, recovery of ancient traditions and culture was difficult. In addition, the vast number of slaves brought to the Near East from Central Asia in the conquests served to dilute the hold of local culture and traditions on those slaves, who encountered another world. When some returned to Central Asia they brought various foreign values with them, which only served to enhance the existing internationalism or cosmopolitanism of Central Asia under an Islamic veneer.

Even though the aristocracy and the intellectuals in Central Asian society were decimated, many joined the Arabs and became instrumental in forging a new Islamic culture beyond the values and mores of Arab tribesmen. Also the mercantile population of Central Asia, accustomed to accept foreign rule as long as the rulers could protect the trade routes and their business, accepted Islam much more readily than the communities of Iran, more bound to their land and to local trade.

Furthermore, the Persian language had become the *lingua franca* for the Muslim armies in the east, and it was not so difficult for the Sogdians and others to learn Persian. In

Tokharistan, Persian was more used than in Sogdiana, even before the Islamic conquests, which is one reason why al-Biruni only knew about Khwarazmian and Sogdian ancient calendars and customs. Tokharistan had become Persianized and lost its ancient culture long before the time of al-Biruni. The Sasanian refugees in Central Asia also provided an impetus for the spread of the Persian language.

While we have spoken about the powerful effects of the conquests and Islam on the people of Central Asia, influences also went the other way. Arabs learned Persian and wore local clothes and styles, and undoubtedly trading partnerships were formed in Central Asia between Arabs, Persians and Sogdians. In the time of Nasr ibn Sayyar Arabic was introduced as the official written language in Khurasan, long after it had spread throughout the rest of the caliphate. Local scribes were quick to see advantages in using Arabic as a much more flexible tool for writing, and for business transactions, than either Sogdian or Persian in its archaic or Pahlavi form. The writing of Persian (i.e. new Persian) in the Arabic alphabet came later in the tenth century, and it first flourished in Central Asia rather than in Iran.

It often has been said that the Arab kingdom of the Umayyads became an Iranian Empire under the 'Abbasids. The 'Abbasid army of Khurasan had been instrumental in overthrowing the Umayyads, and with the capital moved from Damascus to Baghdad, a new era came into being in Iran and Central Asia. For a new Islamic culture was being forged in Khurasan and Transoxiana, as well as in Baghdad where many people from Khurasan and Transoxiana settled, which would have repercussions all over the Islamic world.

## Notes

1. Writings about the Arabs in the east concentrate on inter-tribal conflicts in Khurasan, such as the classic work by J. Wellhausen, *Das Arabische Reich und sein Sturz* (Berlin: Reiner, 1902), and H. Gibb, *The Arab Conquests in Central Asia* (London: Royal Asiatic Society, 1923). The Central Asians receive much better coverage in the writings of W. Barthold, especially his *Turkestan down to the Mongol Invasion* (London: Luzac, 1968), and by R.

Frye, *The Golden Age of Persia* (London: Weidenfeld & Nicolson, 1975). Specifically on the early conquests in Central Asia cf. G. Goibov, *Rannye pokhody Arabov v Sredyuyu Aziyu* (Dushanbe: Donish, 1989).

2. For discussion of the name with further references see W. Sundermann, "An Early Attestation of the Name of the Tajiks," in W. Skalmowski, ed., *Medioiranica* (Leuven: Peeters, 1993), 163–71.

# CHAPTER 15

# The Iranian-Islamic Œcumene

With the establishment of the 'Abbasid Caliphate, several changes become apparent in Khurasan and Central Asia. The end of influence on political events by the Arab tribes is the most striking change from Umayyad times. This does not mean that the Arab tribes left Khurasan, or they no longer existed in the east, but they had lost their organization and their importance. Many had been assimilated into the settled population, and the term *mawali*, as clients of a tribe, is no longer found in the sources. We now speak only of Muslims or non-Muslims, but as more and more people converted to Islam a new pattern of differentiation became apparent. In the east it came to be based on language: first between Arabs, together with Arabicized converts, and Iranians who even after conversion really did not learn Arabic; later we find a distinction between Iranians and Turks. The disputes between Arab, or Arabicized, and Iranian literati, called *Shu'ubiyya,* which took place in Baghdad, and elsewhere in Iran, were unimportant for Central Asia.

Another change was that the Arab conquests brought the various Iranian speaking peoples together in one political unit, the caliphate, for the first time since the Achaemenid Empire. Sasanian, as well as Arab, influences came to Central Asia, but Islam provided a much stronger glue than anything previous. The new Persian language that spread in Iran and Central Asia was not simply the old dialect of Fars province, nor even that form of it enriched by Parthian and other elements, which was the official language of the Sasanian Empire, called *dari* by later writers, after the Persian word for the court. The new Persian language of the eastern part of the caliphate was now enriched with Sogdian, and other words and expressions, even though the basic grammar remained the dialect of Fars. Other dialects, of course, abounded, even as they do down to the present. What happened in Transoxiana, however, became important for the whole eastern part of the caliphate.

Another change was the removal of the governorship of Khurasan from Iraq. Henceforth the governor of Khurasan was responsible only to the caliph in Baghdad, and as time passed the governor became more independent. His officials were sent to various regions of the east, and they gradually replaced the local rulers, who were relegated to the aristocracy or *dihqan* class. Also Merv lost its important position as the base of Arab campaigns across the river, for it no longer occupied the strategic position it had held under the Umayyads. More often the governor of Khurasan preferred Nishapur as his capital, although at times other towns were selected for this honor. The governor, like the caliph in Baghdad, was addressed as *amir*, which title assumed a general meaning of commander or ruler. The provincial courts copied Baghdad and became miniatures of the caliphal capital in many respects. Perhaps the most obvious parallel between the caliphal court and the governor's administration, since it figures so prominently in the sources, was the prime minister or *vezir* in both. Disputes exist about the origin of the word, whether Arabic or Persian, but at any rate, the institution and its trappings were copied from the Sasanian office of prime minister to the ruler.

The organization of the central government in Baghdad under the 'Abbasids cannot be detailed here, but inasmuch as local institutions were modelled on those of the capital, we may refer to the center to elucidate missing information in the provinces. Although Transoxiana remained under the jurisdiction of the governor of Khurasan, local districts usually maintained their previous position, if not their autonomy. Although circumstances varied in different regions, a general picture may be reconstructed. An oasis would be governed by a *wali* or sub-governor, usually appointed by the governor of the large province (*amir*), or rarely directly from Baghdad. Beside the *wali* would be an *'amil* or tax collector, a postmaster, and a *qadi* or judge, all appointed by the provincial governor. The towns had their own organization, with a *ra'is* or mayor as head of the urban organization. In Central Asia this office became more important than elsewhere in the caliphate, where officials sent from Baghdad to represent central governmental interests frequently dominated the city government. Corruption, with the buying and selling of posts, was rampant everywhere and at all levels. In the towns of Central Asia the merchants retained their prominent positions, and the towns became organized with guilds, and quarters of towns headed by *shaikhs,* who also attended to such matters as municipal problems of supplies, wastes, and education. A new element entered the picture, however, and that was the religious establishment of *qadis* and *mullahs,* or religious leaders.

It is difficult to reconstruct the rise in importance of the legal schools and their scholars in the towns of Central Asia, since there does not seem to have been any precedent for this new phenomenon. In Bukhara the leaders of the Hanafite school of jurisprudence triumphed over the Hanbali, Shafi'i and Maliki schools. We read that in other towns intra-urban warfare broke out between partisans of one or the other school. In Nishapur the fighting between the Hanafis and Shafi'is over power in the city government ruined the city.

The union of religion and state in one person, the caliph, was quite new for the Central Asians, but they seem to have adopted it with alacrity, for it was in Bukhara, Samarkand, Balkh, and other centers of Central Asia that the transformation of Islamic culture from an Arab to a universal culture took place. Baghdad, of course, was important as the capital, but it was a new foundation filled with Khurasanis, as well as others from all over the caliphate. And the caliph had religious as well as secular authority, which the governors lacked.

Let us first look at the religious situation. Universal Islam, culturally speaking, was born at the beginning of the 'Abbasid Caliphate in the midst of a welter of heretical and syncretic religious movements that had been absent from the earlier period. Many revolts arose at the end of the Umayyad Caliphate, when everywhere there were uprisings against the government, and most had religious dimensions. The uprisings were a sign of religious as well as political ferment in the east, and the leaders of most sought the support of the lower classes, who were ready to follow any messiah who promised release from their misery. We have records of a number of these movements, and always social and political factors are present as well as religious.[1]

Zoroastrian communities existed in Khurasan, and they too were rent by opposition to the orthodox priesthood, which had survived from Sasanian times. One Zoroastrian priest called Bihafrid, who acquired a following in Nishapur and vicinity, was attacked by the orthodox Zoroastrian community, who asked Abu Muslim to arrest and execute the heretic, which he did in 749. Another Zoroastrian priest, called Sunpad or Sinbad, raised a revolt after the death of Abu Muslim, claiming to revenge his assassination at the instigation of the 'Abbasid caliph Mansur, but he was defeated and later killed. It is first with Sunpad, and then with another rebel, Ishaq the Turk, several years later, that we see a joining of Islamic and Zoroastrian beliefs in expectation of a messiah. Many Shi'ite partisans, who felt betrayed by the seizure of power by the 'Abbasids, in place of a member of the family of 'Ali, also believed that a messiah or *mahdi* would lead them to victory over the 'Abbasids. Various opponents of the 'Abbasids would join forces, and the result would be difficult to identify. The confusion of religious beliefs and political propaganda in these early movements is apparent.

Another religious-political revolt that broke out in Badghis, led by a professed follower of Bihafrid called Ustad Sis, attained a large following, which continued to exist after his capture and execution in 768. All of these rebels had non-Islamic names except Ishaq, but the next revolts seem to have been instigated by Muslims. Yusuf ibn Ibrahim, called al-Barm, raised a banner of opposition in Sistan, but he went to Bukhara, where he succeeded in attracting a group of people who called themselves adherents of the Khurramdin "happy" religion, a synthesis of Muslim and Zoroastrian beliefs. His followers too continued to exist after the capture and execution of their leader in 778. From 775 to 783 another religious figure called Muqanna', "the veiled prophet," secured a large following in Nasaf and Kesh of Sogdiana, as well as from the villages of Bukhara. He claimed to be a reincarnation of Abu Muslim, and his followers wore white garments in opposition to the black colors of the 'Abbasids. He too was defeated and killed, but his followers continued to exist after his death. Some of these religious insurrections were called revivals of the Mazdakites, a religio-social movement of the time of the Sasanian Kavad, but any actual connection is difficult to establish.

It is not possible to reconcile the various accounts of each of these movements, which tell of dualism, metempsychosis, and other beliefs. Suffice it to say that the proliferation of religious, political, and/or social groups in Khurasan, including Transoxiana, under the early 'Abbasids parallels the many different tendencies in the Christian religion of the first few centuries of our era. The social character of most of the movements is obvious, since they appealed to the masses. In Central Asia, on the frontier of the caliphate, not only could heretics survive, but Christians and Manichaeans could pursue missionary activities further into the far reaches of Central Asia. Some of the movements are said to have had their roots in pre-Islamic times, which is possible, but information about them is unavailable.

Mainstream Muslims were not loath to follow suit in uprisings, but their approach was different from the other religions, since their motives for opposition were more political than religious. Although there had been attempts to convert the whole population to Islam under the Umayyads, by promising a release from taxation for new converts, this deliverance was not carried through. In 728 such an attempt by Ashras, a governor of Khurasan, caused not a conciliation but rather a revolt by various groups.

By the time of the 'Abbasid Caliphate Islam had spread, while the principles or pillars of Islam were still being formulated. One of them was the *jihad* or holy war against infidels. The tradition of raiding, which was so characteristic of the early Arab advances in Central Asia, was not forgotten, and under the 'Abbasids a Muslim could combine his Islamic

*Figure 20.* Kabul, silver coins of Nezak and other rulers in
northern Afghanistan, 8th–9th cent.

*Figure 21.* Reverses of the coins above

duty with hope for booty. The Central Asian frontier of Islam attracted warriors for the faith, like the Byzantine frontier and Spain. And just as on those two frontiers heroes appeared on both sides, so also in Central Asia.

The Cid in Spain and Diogenes Akritas in Anatolia engendered stories about their exploits which have survived, but in Central Asia we have only a few names, and no surviving literature about the struggles between Muslims and infidels. Later, Budrach, apparently one of the heroes on the Uighur Buddhist side fighting against the Muslim Karakhanids of Kashgar, seems to have followed the same career as the Cid. Many times in Arabic writings we hear of *ghazis*, as the warriors for Islam were called, who gathered in the spring at *ribats,* or fortified villas, to go on expeditions principally against the Turks in the steppes, but also into the mountains where Islam had not penetrated.

At the same time Transoxiana was not immune to raids by pagan Turks from the north, and the governors of Khurasan, together with local authorities, repaired and extended the walls around not only the towns, but also entire oases in Transoxiana. This "wall psychology," as we have seen, dominated the policies of Central Asian governments from the time of the Seleucids down to the ʿAbbasid Caliphate. The Sasanians had also built long walls on the plains of northern Gurgan, and in the Caucasus at Derbent, but their effectiveness, both in Iran and in Central Asia, was questionable. It was not until the tenth century, in the time of Ismail, the Samanid ruler of Transoxiana, that the oasis walls of Bukhara and Samarkand were abandoned as no longer necessary. Other oases also seem to have abandoned long defensive walls at this time, perhaps an indication of the walls' ineffectiveness against nomads.

By the end of the ninth century Islam had made great progress in western Central Asia, whereas in Iran the countryside remained Zoroastrian for over a century later. The impetus to spread Islam into the villages of Iran came from Shiʿite Ismaili missionaries, sent from Fatimid Egypt at the outset of the tenth century, whose efforts were just as much directed against Sunni Muslims, recognized by the state, as against non-Muslims. The state, in response, supported its own Sunni missionaries. In Central Asia, however, the sectarians made little headway, in part because such towns as Bukhara, Balkh and Samarkand had already become fountainheads of Sunni Islamic learning.

It is significant that we hear of many Islamic savants called Bukhari, Balkhi, Samarkandi, or Termezi in the first century of 'Abbasid rule, but few Shirazis or Isfahanis. One could almost speak of a Bukhara-Baghdad axis in Islamic learning. In Iran conversion was slower than in Central Asia, and the majority of the population on the land remained Zoroastrian, Christian or Jewish, whereas in Central Asia the majority became Muslim, hence Islamic learning blossomed there. The geographer al-Muqaddasi wrote that in the east (of Iran) scholars (*'ulama*) were valued, while in Shiraz (and the west) scribes were esteemed.[3]

Zoroastrian influences on Islam came from Iran, while any supposed Buddhist connections would be from Tokharistan. It is highly controversial whether the Islamic mystical, or even ascetic, movement called Sufism derived any impetus from Buddhism. One of the early Sufis was Ibrahim ibn Adham of Balkh (d. 777), and the school he established had features reminiscent of the asceticism of Buddhist monks. Balkh at the time of the Arab conquests had been a center of Buddhism, with a famous *vihara* called Naubahar in the Arabic sources. In the realm of religion this seems to be the most likely possible contribution of pre-Islamic Central Asia to the Islamic faith.

It was the army of Khurasan that overthrew the Umayyad Caliphate, and the 'Abbasids maintained close connections with the east, especially in trade and commerce, which expanded enormously. The old Sogdian merchant trade routes to the east now started to see merchants who identified themselves as Muslims. The prophet Muhammad and his wife and friends had been merchants, and Islam was an urban culture, which fitted better with Central Asian conceptions than with Iranian. But prosperity was not limited to Central Asia; it spread throughout the caliphate. The merchants of Central Asia were busy in various parts of the caliphate, and in their own way bringing east and west together in the oecumene of Islam. Another realm of the consolidation of Iran and Central Asia was the fine arts.

It is probable that later Islamic miniature painting, depicting human forms, drew some inspiration from the wall paintings and the books of Manichaean miniatures in Central Asia, for the tradition of art in late Sasanian Iran was mainly floral and geometrical. The depiction of humans in miniatures of the 'Abbasid era from Iraq is quite different from the later specimens in the east, which is not unexpected. The absence of any examples of early eastern Islamic miniatures is puzzling, for figures do appear on ceramics from Nishapur and elsewhere in the east. Nonetheless, Islamic art was receiving its distinctive features as part of the Islamic civilization being formed. But the ramifications of art motifs are complicated, and there are many questions unanswered, such as the presumed eastern Iranian or Central Asian origin of the *eyvan* form of architecture, the artistic background for episodes of stories depicted in Islamic miniatures, and others. For the myriad of details about motifs and decorations, transmission of influences, and the like, the reader is referred to the works of art historians in this field.[4]

I do not intend here to write about the weakening of 'Abbasid authority in the east or the rise of Iranian dynasties—first the Tahirids, then the Saffarids and finally the Samanids—for others have done so in detail.[5] Nonetheless, since it was under the Samanids that the brilliant eastern Islamic culture came to fruition, a few words should be said about this last Iranian dynasty in Central Asia.

The ancestor of the family, from whom came the name, was said to have been a *dihqan* who lived in a village near the town of Termez. After accepting Islam at the beginning of 'Abbasid rule, he and his son Asad gained prominence locally. But his four grandsons acquired important positions from the Tahirid governor of Khurasan for their aid in support of the caliph Ma'mun. About 820 Nuh, the eldest of the brothers, was appointed sub-governor of Samarkand, Ahmad was sent in the same capacity to Ferghana, Yahya to Shash and

Ilyas to Herat. The eldest brother was considered head of the family, and when Nuh died in 842 his brother Ahmad took the position of seniority in the family. He sent his son Nasr to rule Samarkand.

Meanwhile the Tahirids, as well as Ilyas in Herat, had been overthrown by an upstart chieftain, Ya'qub "the Coppersmith," in 873, and the Samanids were now able to assert their independence from Khurasan. To make a long story short, Nasr sent his brother Ismail to Bukhara, and after many vicissitudes Ismail became head of the family and Bukhara became the capital of a new dynasty of the Samanids in 892.

Ismail consolidated his power in Transoxiana by making treaties with local lords, or by appointing his relatives to various towns. In 900 he defeated and captured 'Amr, successor to Ya'qub, and then received from the caliph in Baghdad appointment over the entire east. We cannot describe his expeditions against the Turks and his conquests in Iran, for a history of the Samanids may be found elsewhere. The significance of Samanid rule in Central Asia, however, should be briefly sketched.

The Samanids were ardent supporters of Sunni Islam, except for a brief interlude of flirtation by Nasr, grandson of Ismail, with Ismaili missionaries. They were also great patrons of Islamic learning, and it was during their rule of a century in Transoxiana that out of the general Islamic culture, a branch of it, what may be called Iranian Islam, began to grow. The Persian language spread under them, even though Arabic remained the official written language of the dynasty. Just as in late Medieval Europe when local tongues were developing, while Latin continued as the primary written language, so in Transoxiana and Khurasan Persian came to be written together with Arabic. The local aristocracy was satisfied that Ismail, one of their own, was ruling, who had sanctioned the joining of old Central Asian traditions with Islam. The old society continued with an Islamic garb. It is ironic that the Samanids—by their conversion of Turkish tribesmen and the intensification of the ancient system of *chakars*, now court slaves—laid the foundations for their own

230

fall. These court slaves were primarily Turks who had been trained to lead armies and to rule.

In Baghdad Turkish slave soldiers came to dominate the central government, and the same happened in Bukhara. First only the military sector was involved, but then the entire state structure. Unlike the caliphal court in Baghdad, however, the Samanids did not have the religious component, to rally the people behind them in the face of a Turkish Karakhanid army. So at the turn of the millennium Central Asia not only was an important Islamic land, but also became the Turkish center of rule, from which Muslim Turks spread to the Balkans and to Delhi. While rule belonged to the Turks, the culture was Iranian, both under the banner of Islam.

It is clear that the Iranian-Islamic oecumene was in place by the year 1000, and influences from it were to spread throughout the entire Islamic world. But that Islamic unity of the 'Abbasid Caliphate, engendered by the Arabic language, was to divide in the future between the eastern and the western Islamic areas, the first using Persian as its literary vehicle, the other retaining Arabic. Perhaps unexpectedly, though it was the Arabs who brought Iran and Central Asia together, the Turks were the principal agents for spreading what we have called the Iranian version of Islamic culture to the west, even to Constantinople.

## Notes

1. A classic book on the subject is by G.H. Sadighi, *Les mouvements religieux iraniens au II*ᵉ *et au III*ᵉ *siècle de l'hégire* (Paris, 1938). See also Frye, *The Golden Age of Persia,* 126–149.
2. On the *ghazis* and other questions of military forces in this period, see P. Jürgen, *The State and the Military; The Samanid Case,* Papers on Inner Asia 26 (Bloomington: Indiana University, 1994), with bibliography. See also R. Frye, *Bukhara, The Medieval Achievement* (Norman: Univ. of Oklahoma Press, 1965).
3. J. de Goeje, *Bibliotheca Geographorum Arabicorum* 3 (Leiden: E.J. Brill, 1901), 440.
4. On Central Asian contributions to Islamic art consult the writings of Galina Pugachenkova, Guitty Azarpay, Boris Marshak,

and Oleg Grabar. For the last two see especially Marshak's *Sogdiiskoe Serebro* (Moscow: Nauka, 1971), expanded in German as *Silberschätze des Orients* (Leipzig: Seemann, 1986), and Grabar's *The Formation of Islamic Art* (New Haven: Yale Univ. Press, 1987).

5. See note 2 above.

# CHAPTER 16

# The Present is Born

р-иккита шеърлари
) ва 1925 йилларда
батларимиз қалби
ва санъатнинг сехр
за чин маънода уст
арларини ўқиб бор
дабий машқларимн

The steppes and eastern Central Asia have been neglected, but the future face of all of the area was determined by the last great movement of peoples to the south, so that we speak of the heartland of Central Asia as eastern and western Turkestan. How did the Turks change the population here?[1] We must go back a little in our treatment of the Turks.

Turkish tribesmen had infiltrated the oasis states of eastern and western Central Asia early in the first millennium of our era, but we have little tangible evidence of this, except in the Chinese dynastic annals, which tell of invasions and conflicts rather than settlements of Turks in the oases. Until the occupation of Turfan, Komul and other oases by the Uighurs, we do not find a settled culture which might be termed Turkish, for before the ninth century the Turkish tribes were nomadic or pastoral. Not that Turks did not settle in towns, especially in the Ili and Chu valleys, but authority and power remained in the hands of the tribal leaders. The Turks were not alone, however, in their depredations into, and eventual settling down in, eastern Turkestan.

Another people who played a role on the stage of history of Xinjiang were the Tibetans, who for more than a century from the 660s fought the Chinese for control of the oasis states.[2] They allied at times with the Turks, but they never established effective control over the area for any length of time. Notices in Arabic sources of Tibetans active in Transoxiana or Tokharistan do not refer to troops of the Tibetan empire with its capital in Lhasa, but rather to mountain peoples of the Karakorum and Himalayas. For the Muslims, the term "Tibetan" was a general descriptive term applied to the highland populations of northern India, possibly only those with Mongolian features. It was the Turks who dominated the scene in the east, to whom we now return.

235

We have already mentioned the defeat of the Hephthalites by forces of what generally is called the first Turkish *Kaghanate,* after which local Turkish dynasties came into existence, the most notable of which was the kingdom of the Turkish *Shahis* of Kabul, which probably was founded towards the end of the seventh century. Before that time, however, there seems to have been a mixture of Turks with Iranian speaking groups among the Hephthalites. Nonetheless the Khalaj Turks are the earliest recorded Turkish pastoralists living in the mountains of Afghanistan. Their origin is most uncertain, although several Arabic and Persian sources claim they are descended from the Hephthalites, but they played little role in the history of this time. The chief opponents of the Arabs in their conquests in Transoxiana were the Türgesh, nominally under the first Turkish *Kaghanate* centered in Mongolia and the Altai region. They were replaced by the Karluks about 766, when a Karluk confederacy came into being.

The second Turkish *Kaghanate*, which had flourished with such notable leaders as Tonyukuk, Kültegin and Bilgä *kaghan* at the beginning of the eighth century, did not last long, and the Uighurs assumed the mantle of the leading power in Mongolia and on the steppes in 744. In the west the Karluks disputed their rule, and hostilities between the two for supremacy over all Turkish tribes continued until the Kirghiz destroyed the Uighur state in Mongolia in 840. Some Turkish tribes, however, remained outside of this struggle, the most prominent of which were the Oghuz or Ghuzz, who roamed east of the Caspian Sea to the Syr Darya. It was both the Oghuz and the Karluks who fought the Muslims, and who then accepted Islam in the tenth century.

The Uighurs did not vanish, after their defeat in Mongolia, but appear in the southern oasis states of the Tarim basin after 840. Already in the north, about 760 their *kaghan*, called Mou-yü in Chinese writings, had accepted Manichaeism from the Sogdians. A southern outpost town, Beshbalik, just east of present Urumqi, became a new capital for the settled Uighurs, who later changed their religion, accepting Buddhism. The Uighurs may have been absorbed by the Tokharians of Kucha and other oases in the northern rim of the Tarim Basin, but they gave their language to the local inhabitants. By the end of the millennium the Turkification of eastern Turkestan was well under way.

At the same time the Karluk confederation of tribes in the western part of Central Asia experienced internal struggles between various tribes, called Yaghma and Chigil, the end result of which at the end of the tenth century was the acceptance of Islam by many tribesmen, and the founding of a state called the Karakhanid, or the domain of the Ilek Khans, both designations remaining enigmatic. The founder of the new state, and the first chieftain to convert to Islam, was called Satuk Bughra Khan in several sources, and he is said to have conquered Kashgar which became the first center of the Karakhanids.

It is not our intention here to describe the history of the Karakhanids or other Turkish dynasties in Central Asia. The Karakhanids waged war against the Buddhist Uighurs to the east, and Islam did not take over Uighur territory until the Mongol period, when Turkish dialects had replaced all of the old languages of eastern Turkestan. In western Central Asia, on the other hand, Turkish tongues did not eliminate the Persian language which prevailed in the towns, especially in Khojent, Samarkand and Bukhara. And just as in Azerbaijan, the process of Turkification was not universal in the countryside. In the Ferghana valley, in the mountains east of Tashkent, and elsewhere Persian speaking villagers continued to live down to the present. In the mountains, relics of Sogdian and other ancient Iranian languages also continue to exist today.

So it was the spread of Islam, more than that of the Turks, which gave Central Asia its future face down to the present. The Samanids were the last Iranian dynasty to rule in Central Asia, and the year 1000 marks the end of the Samanid dynasty, but the Iranian-Islamic culture was not replaced by a Turkish-Islamic civilization. Rather the Islamic Turkish literature, which began under the Karakhanids, and had its roots in Iranian conventions, was then absorbed into the Persian literary tradition, while the non-Islamic literature and culture of the Uighurs in the east represented the last manifestation of the ancient heritage of Central Asia, until it too vanished under the Islamic wave.

At the beginning of the twentieth century, if one wished to characterize the culture of Central Asia, the western part was an extension of the Near Eastern, Islamic world, while the east, although similar, had a thick Sinicized veneer, which was penetrating ever deeper. Politically, of course, western Central Asia was part of the Russian Empire while the eastern side belonged to the Chinese Empire.

At the end of the century, with the Soviet Union in pieces under the onslaught of Western (that is, modern, technological) civilization, all of Central Asia, in many local conflicts, was seeking to recover its past and its identity face to face with an even stronger challenge: the one world of multinational companies and technology. The two attractions, one towards unity with the rest of the world, and the other national identity, pulling in opposite directions, threaten to turn Central Asia into a region of chaos and instability. The resolution of, or compromise between, the two trends is essential to the future of Central Asia. Of course, this is a problem not only for Central Asians but for many others in the world, and so far the most successful resolution of the difficulty has been realized by the Japanese. However, many claim that in Japan the process of balancing two cultures has resulted in a cultural split personality, while others retort that such a state of affairs is not a curse but a blessing.

The reconciliation of local cultures with a world culture is indeed one of the great challenges of the future, and Central Asia is passionately involved in it. Only time will tell whether people have resolved this dilemma, among the myriad other problems which beset the future world.

## Notes

1. I do not intend to discuss Central Asian Turkish history, which is a vast subject, but to complete the ancient elements, bringing them to post-Islamic times, it is necessary to briefly consider the Turkish factor. For further reading consult the various chapters

of D. Sinor, ed., *The Cambridge History of Early Inner Asia,* op. cit.

2. The book by C. Beckwith, *The Tibetan Empire in Central Asia* (Princeton, 1987), gives a good survey of Tibetan activity to the north of Tibet, but it overstates their conquests and diplomacy to the west of their plateau.

# Appendices

## Appendix 1: The Literary Sources

Chinese sources for the pre-Han and early Han dynasty include the *Shih-chi,* which has been translated into English by B. Watson, *Records of the Grand Historian of China*, 2 vols. (New York: Columbia Univ. Press, 1961). The history of the former Han dynasty is the *Ch'ien Han Shu,* written by Pan Ku about 90 C.E., and also translated into English by H. Dubs, *The History of the Former Han Dynasty,* 3 vols. (Baltimore-Wash.: ACLS, 1944). The *Hou Han Shu*, or account of the later Han dynasty, was compiled by Fan-yeh about 440 C.E., using the same information about western countries that is found in the *Shih-chi* and the *Ch'ien Han Shu.* A French translation was made by Chavannes, "Les pays d'occident d'après le heou han chou," *T'oung Pao* 8 (Leiden, 1907), esp. 191–95.

For the post-Kushan and Hephthalite period, information is scarce. Later Chinese dynastic accounts add little new information, except at times mentioning embassies sent to China by the western states. Furthermore, in regard to the western regions, the late *Wei Shu* copies the *Pei Shih,* which in turn reproduces the *Chou Shu.* For a translation and analysis of the last see R.A. Miller, *Accounts of the Western Nations in the History of the Northern Chou Dynasty* (Berkeley: Univ. of California Press, 1959). For a detailed discussion of the geography of the western regions down to the T'ang dynasty, see L. Borovkova, *Zapad Tsentral'noi Azii vo II v. do n.e.–VII v. n.e.* (Moscow: Nauka, 1989).

During the Sui period, and even more during the following T'ang dynasty, new knowledge of the west comes to China. Fortunately we have translations of the relevant texts in French and Russian, such as the reprint of the classic by E. Chavannes, *Documents sur les Tou-Kiue (Turcs) occidentaux* (Paris: A. Maisonneuve, 1946), and the reprint of the somewhat outdated Y. Bichurin, *Sobranie svedenii o narodakh, obitavshikh v Sredne Azii,* 3 vols. (Moscow, 1950–53). A good commentary on the information found in the T'ang history is in A. G. Malyavkin, *Tanskie Khroniki o gosudarstvakh tsentralnoi Azii* (Novosibirsk: Nauka otd., 1989).

Classical sources are easily located, in either the Tuebner (Leipzig) or Loeb (Cambridge, Mass.) series, plus F. Jacobi, ed., *Die Fragmente der griechischen Historiker* (FrGH), 3 vols. (Berlin: Weidemann, 1954–64). Byzantine writers who mention Central Asia are Ammianus, Menander Protektor, and Theophanes, whose texts can be found in the old corpus of Byzantine historians, or in many later editions and translations.

Arabic writings that contain materials on Central Asia are historians such as Tabari, now translated into English, Baladhuri's story of the conquests, Ya'qubi and Atham al-Kufi, and many geographers. In Persian, Narshakhi's *History of Bukhara,* transl. R. Frye (Cambridge, Mass.: Mediaeval Society, 1954), is the best town history in Central Asia. On all of these Islamic sources, cf. W. Barthold, *Turkestan down to the Mongol Invasion,* op. cit. Although the Samanids, especially Ismail, are praised in many literary and other works, there exists no separate history of the dynasty comparable to histories of later dynasties.

# Appendix 2: Geographical Names

*Ancient or Medieval names in Central Asia*
*with modern equivalents*

The following identifications are only approximate, since sites of towns have changed from antiquity to the present, but the general area of each town is meant.

There was no general name for Central Asia in ancient times, but the Arabs designated the land south of the Oxus (present Amu Darya) as Khurasan and lands to the north as *ma wara' l-nahr*, "the other side of the river."

Bactria (O.P. *Baktrish*, medieval Balkh) was the land on both sides of the Oxus in what today is northern Afghanistan, southern Uzbekistan and Tajikistan south of the Hissar mountain range. Although we have ancient place names in Ptolemy, Strabo and elsewhere, there is no clear delineation of districts or subdivisions of the land until medieval Islamic times. Although names changed, one may suppose that the geographical divisions remained constant, even though the political boundaries at times covered several geographical areas. We find approximately the following subdivisions in the Arabic geographies, testimony to the existence of many small kingdoms in valleys between the mountains:

| ANCIENT NAME | MODERN NAME |
|---|---|
| Tokharistan | Badakhshan |
| Tirmidh | Termez |
| Chaganiyan | Surkhan Darya valley |
| Akharun | western part of Hissar valley |
| | on banks of present Shirkent Darya |
| Shuman | Dushanbe area |
| Kobadian | lower course of Kafirnigan River |
| Khalaverd | Kafir Kaleh near Kurgan Tiube |
| | in the Vakhsh valley |
| Rasht | Ab-i Garm or Karategin |
| Khuttalan | capital at Vose near Kulob |
| Khulbuk | Kurbanshahid |
| Vakhsh | near Kurgan Tiube |

Guftan and Buzgala were names given to the area by the "Iron Gate" near the present Sherabad River.

Ancient Sogdiana, or present Uzbekistan north of the Hissar range, had the following districts:

| ANCIENT NAME | MODERN NAME |
|---|---|
| Nakhshab or Nasaf | Karshi |
| Kesh | Shahrisabz |
| Maimurgh | probably Urgut |
| Panj | Panjikant |
| Marakanda or Afrasiyab | Samarkand |
| Bukhara | as today |
| Paikand and Firabr near the Amu Darya in the oasis of Bukhara | as at present |
| Chach or Shash | Tashkent |
| Bunjikath | left bank of Shahristan River near Ura Tiube |
| Bashgird | Faizabad |
| Ustrushana | Ura Tiube and east to Khojent |
| Ilak | an area to the east of Chach |
| Isfijab | to the north of Chach |
| towns of Farab or Otrar | in the area of present Chimkent |
| town of Taraz or Talas | east of Dzhambul |
| Balasaghun | in the Chu valley |
| Suyab | on the Chu River |

The towns of Ishtikhan and Kushaniya were in the fertile valley west of Samarkand and north of the Zarafshan River, which is called Miankala at present. On the middle of the Syr Darya was the first capital of the Chach region, called Kanka, later Kharajket.

It should be noted that several towns were called Bunjikath or Bunkat, the latter sometimes applied to present Tashkent.

The eastern part of the Ferghana valley had a number of towns, such as:

| ANCIENT NAME | MODERN NAME |
|---|---|
| Uzkand | near Jalalabad in Kirgizia |
| Akhsikath | west of Namangan |
| Kasan | a village on a river to the north of Namangan |
| Kuba | to the west of Osh |
| Andijan and Osh | as today |

As streams changed their courses the sites of settlements also varied.

Khwarazm, or present Karakalpakia, was located on both sides of the lower Amu Darya where its delta entered the Aral Sea. The old capital was Kath, on the east side of the Oxus, while Gurganj and Hazarasp were to the west of the river. Other more ancient sites, known by modern names such as Janbas Kaleh, Koi Krylgan Kaleh, and Toprak Kaleh, are on the sands to the east of the river and southeast of the Aral Sea.

For further information see the classic by G. Le Strange, *Lands of the Eastern Caliphate* (Cambridge: Cambridge Univ. Press, 1930 reprint), and V. Minorsky, *Hudud al-'Alam* (London: Luzac, 1937).

In Xinjiang or east Turkestan archaeological sites are easier to locate since the oases remained constant throughout history, while only the extensions of now-dry streams into the desert of the Tarim basin reveal ancient towns buried in the sand. The sites are shown on map C.

I have used the adjectives Turkic and Turkish interchangeably, although some scholars employ Turkic for eastern and Turkish for Anatolian Turks.

## Appendix 3: Local rulers in
## Bukhara and Samarkand

For a fuller list of rulers of various western Central Asian principalities, with Chinese characters and transcriptions, and with Sogdian and Arabic forms where known, see O.I. Smirnova, *Svodnyi Katalog Sogdiiskikh Monet, bronza* (Moscow: Nauka, 1981), 423–30.

In Samarkand the following rulers are known from Sogdian legends on coins: Shishpir (ca. 640–660), followed by Varguman for a few years, then no ruler. From ca. 680 to 700, Doaspad and Nineshis. From 700 to 712, Tarkhun, and from 712 to 737 Ghurak, with two years of Devashtich, when Ghurak had abandoned Samarkand. Turgar, who ruled to ca. 740, is the last ruler whose name is known.

In Bukhara the coins do not have the names of rulers, but from Islamic sources we find the following: Shaba (?), ca. 655–60; Bidun, ca. 660–680; Khatun, 681 to ca. 693; Doaspad or Tughshada I, 693–727; Tughshada II from 727–738 or 739; Qutaiba, son of Tughshada II, 739–750. Then came Sikan (?), who ruled 10 years, and finally Bunyat, who was killed by order of the Caliph Mahdi in 782 or 783.

It is interesting to note that in Panjikant, from ca. 694 to ca. 708 a Turkish ruler is recorded, Chekin Chur Bilge, successor of Gamaukiyan and predecessor of Devashtich. Cf. V.A. Livshits, "Praviteli Pendzhikenta VII–nachala VIII v.," in P.A. Gryaznevich, ed., *Pis'mennye pamyatniki i problemy istorii i kul'tury narodov vostoka* (Moscow: Nauka, 1977), 109–121, also in Livshits's "Praviteli Pancha" in *Narody Azii i Afriki*, 1979, no. 4. For other regions the lack of coinage with names of rulers prevents reconstructions.

# Appendix 4: Deities in Sogdiana

In addition to adherents of the Christian, Manichaean and Buddhist religions, followers of Indian cults were also present, whether worshipped by Indian merchants or local Sogdians is difficult to determine. On the Siva-Parvati sculpture found in Panjikant see V. Shkoda, "Eine Siva-Heiligtum in Pendzhikent," 25, *Archeologische Mitteilungen aus Iran* (Berlin: Reimer, 1992), 319–27.

Among the local deities were:

| | |
|---|---|
| *'xwrmzt* | Ahura Mazda |
| *nny* | Nana |
| *myr* | Mithra, perhaps earlier called only *baga* |
| *wysh* or *wyshprkr* | Vayu |
| *'rwt* | Haurvatat? |
| *rshn* | Rashnu |
| *r'm* | Raman |
| *y'm'kk* | Yima |
| *'zrw* | Zurvan |
| *wxwshw* | Oxus River |
| *xwm* | haoma |

plus some names possibly of divinities:
*s's'n, drymt, 'prwt, 'by'mn.*

This list is by no means exhaustive.

These deities are mentioned in Sogdian texts, and some are portrayed in wall paintings or in sculptures. For example, Nana, apparently a patron goddess of Panjikant, was depicted in several poses, most frequently seated on a lion.

# Appendix 5: The Languages of Central Asia

ABOUT 50 B.C.E.

| Language | Bactria | Sogdiana | Kashgar | Khotan | Kucha-Turfan |
|---|---|---|---|---|---|
| *official written* | Greek | degenerate Aramaic | Prakrit or Chinese | Prakrit | Chinese |
| *official spoken* | Bactrian | Sogdian or Bactrian | Prakrit or Bactrian | Saka | Tokharian or Chinese |
| *religious* | Avestan or Prakrit | Avestan | Avestan or Prakrit | Prakrit or Sanskrit | Prakrit or Sanskrit |
| *dialect* | Bactrian | Sogdian | "Kanjaki" | Saka | Tokharian B |
| *mercantile* | Parthian ? | Sogdian | Sogdian | Prakrit | Sogdian or Chinese |

## ABOUT 650 C.E.

| Language | Bactria | Sogdiana | Kashgar | Khotan | Kucha | Turfan |
|---|---|---|---|---|---|---|
| *official written* | Bactrian or Persian | Sogdian | Saka or Sogdian | Saka | Chinese & Tokharian B | Chinese & Sogdian ? |
| *official spoken* | Persian | Sogdian | Sogdian | Saka | | |
| *religious* | Avestan or Sanskrit | Avestan, Syriac, or Parthian | Avestan or Sanskrit | Sanskrit or Saka | Prakrit or Sanskrit | Sanskrit, Syriac, or Parthian |
| *dialect* | Bactrian or Persian | Sogdian | "Kanjaki" | Saka | Tokharian B or Tokharian B | Turkic |
| *mercantile* | Persian or Sogdian | Sogdian | Sogdian | Chinese? | Sogdian or Chinese | Sogdian or Chinese |

## SACRED AND PROFANE LANGUAGES

| | "Sacred" oral languages | "Sacred" written languages | Profane written languages |
|---|---|---|---|
| *ca. 50 B.C.E.* | Vedic Sanskrit, Avestan | Sanskrit | Aramaic (degenerate), Greek, Prakrit, Chinese |
| *ca. 650 C.E.* | same as above | Vedic Sanskrit, Avestan, Syriac, Parthian | Sogdian, Khwarazmian, Bactrian, Middle Persian, Saka, Turkic, Tokharian, Chinese |

# Appendix 6: Ancient coinage in Transoxiana

1. In Bactria coins of the central governments, first the Seleucids and then the Greco-Bactrian monarchs, were minted, followed by the coinage of the Kushans, although it is possible that a Saka ruler may have issued coins in Bactria for a short time after the fall of the Greco-Bactrian kingdom. Kidarite and Hephthalite coinage followed the issues of the Kushano-Sasanian governors.

2. In Samarkand the earliest coins that were issued were copies of the coinage of Antiochus I, followed by copies of the coinage of Hyrkodes, as well as small silver coins with an archer on them. Shortly before the Arab conquest, Chinese style copper coins (with a square hole in the center) with Sogdian legends were minted in Samarkand.

3. The earliest coinage of the oasis of Bukhara seems to have been copies of the coinage of Euthydemus. In Paikand imitations of Hyrkodes were minted and various copper coins were current in the oasis. The so-called "Bukhar Khudat" coins were struck beginning in the 5th century of our era.

4. In Choresmia copies of the coinage of Eucratides were issued but with a *tamga* (coat-of-arms) of Choresmia on them. Later, several styles of indigenous coinage not obviously copied from a foreign type are found.

5. Kesh and Nasaf apparently first copied Hyrkodes coins but later had their own copper coinage.

6. The first coinage of Chach was late in the 3d century of our era, with an indigenous design and a local *tamga* on them. The style of these copper coins was similar to, but not copied from, Sasanian coins.

7. Later than all of the above-mentioned coinages was that of Ustrushana, of the 7th century, apparently copying Sasanian coins.

8. Even later in time are local coinages of the Ferghana valley, in the 7th and 8th centuries, when we find copies of Chinese, Chach and Sogdian coins.

There were other coins, of course, but the general outline is the above. It will be seen that the striking of coins spread northward from Bactria and the latest examples are from the Ferghana valley.

# Index

253

# Photo Credits

Alphabets and writing styles of Central Asia are illustrated on the title pages of each chapter as follows:

Chapter 1:   Pictographs*
Chapter 2:   Tokharian*
Chapter 3:   Aramaic*
Chapter 4:   Avestan (from Wilhelm Geiger, *Handbuch der Awestasprache*, Erlangen, 1879)
Chapter 5:   Old Persian cuneiform*
Chapter 6:   Greek*
Chapter 7:   Karoshthi*
Chapter 8:   Manichaean*
Chapter 9:   Kushano-Bactrian (from Göbl, *Die drei Versionen der Kaniska-Inschrift von Surkh Kotal,* Österreichische Akademie der Wissenschaften, Denkschrift 88, Vienna, 1965)
Chapter 10: Chinese*
Chapter 11: Khotanese, North Brahmi script (from M. Vorobeva-Desyatovska, *Skazanie o Bxadre Nauka*, Moscow, 1965)
Chapter 12: Turkic runes (from *Inscriptions de l'Orkhon*, Helsingfors, 1892)
Chapter 13: Sogdian*
Chapter 14: Arabic*
Chapter 15: Persian*
Chapter 16: Uzbek (*Uzbek Tili va Adabiëti*, Tashkent, 1989, no. 1)

*From Hans Jensen, *Die Schrift* (Berlin: Deutscher Verlag der Wissenschaften, 1969).

Other illustrations in the text were provided by the author.